Praise fo

"Successful founders, like success_ _____ts coaches, deliver results through people. This book shows you how to do that brilliantly. It is a must-read for every founder."

—Sir Clive Woodward, 2003 Rugby World Cup winning head coach

"Simon and I used the ideas in this book to transform Tipico from a startup into a unicorn, and now he's helping me to build great companies in Europe, Asia, and Africa. The book contains decades of hard-won experience backed up with evidence. If you want to grow as a leader, do yourself a favor and read this book."

—Jan Bolz, former CEO, Tipico; managing partner, IOI Capital

"At last—a leadership book for founders and entrepreneurs instead of corporate managers. The clear structure and layout make this a perfect handbook to keep by your side as well as an easily digestible read from cover to cover. Highly recommended as a practical, no-nonsense guide rooted in hands-on experience usefully combined with the relevant literature."

—Marcus Alexander, adjunct professor of strategy & entrepreneurship, London Business School

"*Founder's Legacy* is an invaluable guide to not just building a great business but also staying sane while doing it. This book captures so much of the hard-fought wisdom that most founders discover only late in their journey, focusing on the challenge of being a founder leader. I highly recommend it no matter if this is your first or tenth founding journey."

—Didier Elzinga, founder & CEO, Culture Amp

"From creating your business to parenting it through the difficult early years to ultimately giving it wings and letting it fly, Simon Court brings humor, wisdom, and decades of experience to this brilliant book. It is bursting with tips, smart questions, and useful references to support you through your founder journey."

—Claire Hynes, co-founder & CEO, Mr. President

"Simon Court's book refocused my perspective on what I had perceived to be limited time to nurture my leadership skills. This book is invaluable. The challenge it gives readers: considerate self-reflection. Perfect for leaders who are busy (Who isn't?) and short on time yet eager to grow themselves and their company. A must-read!"

—Eli Bressert, founder & CEO, Origin

"An essential handbook, packed with real-life stories, for anyone starting or running a purpose-led business. It's not for those who want to make a quick buck; it's for those aiming to create a business with a lasting legacy."

—Alastair Wilson, CEO, School for Social Entrepreneurs

"As an early-stage founder, there always seem more important things to worry about than your own development . . . Reading *Founder's Legacy* has made a practical impact on how I interact with my team and, maybe more importantly, the joy that I get out of running Limbic."

—Sebastiaan de Vries, co-founder & CTO, Limbic AI

"I wish I had read this book ten years ago! Simon makes leadership both tangible and relatable for a founder/CEO. His questions help you to reflect and to put it into practice."

—Maria Raga, former CEO, Depop; angel investor

"One of those rare books from a leader who has successfully trod the path himself but also, with deft humility, advised and supported many others over the course of his long and varied career. As a result, *Founder's Legacy* is full of reflective wisdom—a rich resource that can be read cover-to-cover or dipped into, per your 'challenge of the day,' for inspiration and action-provoking ideas. A founder's legacy indeed!"

—Dom Moorhouse, founder & CEO, Method Grid

"In *Founder's Legacy*, Simon Court delivers fantastic insights and actionable advice for entrepreneurs navigating the myriad leadership challenges of growth. This is all brought to life in a fresh and compelling manner supported by rich stories and engaging case studies."

—Gurnek Bains, founder, Global Future; author of
Meaning, Inc. and *Cultural DNA*

"*Founder's Legacy* is the book every founder and CEO needs. Simon Court not only does an incredible job of dissecting most of the challenges we face but does it with empathy, style, and a sense of fun. Simon was one of the most influential people in my life. In this book, I recognize him in every word he has written; his values shine through every page. Simon is leaving us his own legacy and continues to give us new tools so we can make our world better."

—Jaime Gine, CEO, Amber; co-founder, Carbon Incubator

SIMON COURT

FOUNDER'S LEGACY

Fifty Game-Changing Leadership Lessons
for Building a Great Business

AN INC.
ORIGINAL

An Inc. Original
New York, New York
www.anincoriginal.com

This work is being published under the *An Inc. Original* imprint by an exclusive arrangement with *Inc. Magazine. Inc. Magazine* and the *Inc.* logo are registered trademarks of Mansueto Ventures, LLC. The *An Inc. Original* logo is a wholly owned trademark of Mansueto Ventures, LLC.

Distributed by River Grove Books

Design and composition by Greenleaf Book Group
Cover design by Greenleaf Book Group
Image credits: Figures 14.1, 15.1, 15.2, 16.1, and 16.2 by permission of Value Partnership Ventures Ltd and Value Partnership Ltd; Figures 5.1, 38.1, and 38.2 by permission of The GC Index®; Figure 24.1 by permission of The Chemistry Group.

Publisher's Cataloging-in-Publication data is available.

Paperback ISBN: 978-1-63909-029-7

Hardcover ISBN: 978-1-63909-031-0

eBook ISBN: 978-1-63909-030-3

First Edition

For my daughter, Meghan, a leader in the making

There is a tide in the affairs of men.
Which, taken at the flood, leads on to fortune;
Omitted, all the voyage of their life
Is bound in shallows and in miseries.
On such a full sea are we now afloat,
And we must take the current when it serves,
Or lose our ventures.

—*Julius Caesar,* Act 4 Scene 3, Shakespeare

Contents

Foreword

Transitioning from the role of a founder to a leader and evolving your company from a scrappy startup to a professional company is not an easy task, but I promise you that it is possible and that this book has the keys to not only surviving that transition but also achieving your vision of success, like I did in growing my startup to unicorn status.

My journey as a business founder began amid the excitement of the late 1990s dot-com boom.

I was mesmerized by the incredible growth of these young Internet companies and their CEOs, who seemed like tech rock stars to me. As the technology landscape started to evolve, my co-founder and I saw a huge opportunity: democratize gaming across the globe by distributing games freely over the Internet.

I had been a gamer all my young life and believed that games had the potential to transcend age, gender, and nationality. We established our company, Miniclip, with a mission to "unleash the gamer in everyone" and worked to orchestrate a paradigm shift in the gaming industry—pioneering concepts like free-to-play games and virtual worlds like Club Penguin.

With no outside funding, we successfully built the company over the next eight years into one of the largest entertainment platforms on the Internet, with more than sixty million players—achieving this growth organically and without spending a single dollar on marketing.

Things were quite chaotic internally, like many rapidly growing startups, but our timing had been perfect and that forgave many of our early mistakes.

Then, in 2008 everything changed. The release of the iPhone introduced a tidal wave of change. Initially, it was hard to assess the implications this would have on our business, but it didn't take long for our tech-savvy players to start moving to this new platform, and we needed to follow them. To quote Warren Buffett, "a rising tide floats all boats . . . only when the tide goes out do you discover who's been swimming naked." Our explosive audience growth had masked many underlying problems and inefficiencies at Miniclip. We needed help, and we needed it fast.

Rachel Page, our HR director at the time, understood the enormity of the challenge we faced. She could see how I struggled to zoom out of the details and build a cohesive plan to transform the company from an Internet game publisher to a mobile developer. It was a huge task, and we were running out of time.

Sensing my anguish, she asked me if I had ever worked with an external consultant to get outside advice. Up to this point, I had always felt that outsiders didn't understand our mission; they were from the old legacy businesses we were disrupting. Moreover, how could a consultant, who probably spent most of their time working for city firms, tell me what I needed to do next?

She challenged my views and bet me her next month's pay packet that I would benefit from a meeting with Simon Court.

Naturally, I took the meeting and quickly recognized the benefits Simon could bring to both Miniclip and to me as CEO. He didn't have all the answers, but through a series of carefully crafted questions, which form the backbone of this book, he teased the knowledge out of me, and together we set to work, building a new strategy for Miniclip to pivot into mobile.

Alongside this, Simon helped me recognize that I needed to evolve from being a founder into a leader and, in doing so, turn Miniclip from being a scrappy startup into a more professional company with vertical specialists who could help it transform. This required me to make significant changes to the top team, a decision that I struggled with as the team gave everything to get the company to that stage. Simon helped me realize what had gotten us to that moment would not get us to where we needed to be in the future. He gave me the courage I needed and the data to back up decisions, and through a combination of coaching and new hires, we rebuilt the executive team into one capable of delivering on the future vision.

Those changes set in motion a massive shift in our business, and over the next five years, we successfully captured a significant share of the mobile games market, surpassing everything we had achieved in the past.

In 2015, that led to Miniclip being acquired by Tencent—one of China's most successful technology companies. In the eight years since the acquisition, Miniclip has grown into one of Europe's largest mobile games companies with sixteen games studios, more than four hundred million players, and thirteen hundred employees.

By 2021, I had spent more than twenty years at the helm, so I took some time to reflect on where the company was heading and whether I still had the energy and talent to lead it for the next decade. With tremendous effort from so many hardworking and talented people and Simon's incredibly valuable input, Miniclip achieved a level of success that I couldn't have imagined in my wildest dreams. That moment felt like the right time to hand the reins over to a new CEO, Saad Choudri.

If you are running a fast-growing business and wrestling with similar challenges to those I faced, then *Founder's Legacy* is going to become your ultimate business companion. Simon's fifty lessons are built from his two decades of working as a consultant in fast-growing businesses like mine, and the results that my company has enjoyed are the best illustration of how his coaching insights could help to transform your business.

—**Rob Small,** Founder and President of Miniclip

Becoming a Leader

Being a founder is hard. Being a founder who becomes a great leader is even harder.

The same is true in reverse. Leaders from corporate life don't always make it in the world of the founder.

And yet both face the same challenges and share a similar route to success.

In this book, I share leadership and founder lessons for success. I break down the things I have learned and share the most valuable knowledge and approaches that have transformed the organizations I have worked with.

So, whether your business is a unicorn in the making or a small startup striving to grow, my goal is to make this your source of ideas, reflections, and inspiration. My mission is to help you to grow as a leader and to build a great business—because, for me, success is defined by *you* achieving *your* goal.

MY EXPERIENCE

I have worked as a leadership coach to business founders, leaders, and leadership teams for the past twenty-five years. In many countries. With businesses at different stages of maturity, from startup to reinvention. And in many different sectors including entertainment, biotechnology, technology, travel, insurance, and venture capital. The businesses have been private, backed by venture capital, private equity, or are publicly owned household names. All of this experience is channeled through me to my clients and now into this book. Clients love to benefit from that experience. But on its own, it isn't enough.

Coaching is often done neutrally. The coach asks the questions, and the client provides the answers. But I didn't gather all that experience only to leave it locked away. Leaders are busy people under pressure. I'm not neutral. That's not who I am as a person, and I have learned to bring who I am to what I do. Leaders find my experience and ideas useful, and I want to help them to make progress fast. I want them to act to change their fortunes and to feel emotionally committed to the change. There is no avoiding the difficulties, uncertainties, and hard work required to change something important. But if they believe that what they want is possible, we will find a way together. It is a uniquely personal relationship.

Much of my work is done behind closed doors. People need the space to share their vulnerability in safety and explore new directions without judgment. They are taking the risk, so they should take the credit for any success, and they have to live with the consequences of any failure. It's not about me. Writing this book felt uncomfortable at first for that very reason. My clients experience me as generous, empathetic, and clear-sighted. I bring insights into the complex relationship between people and business. I tell them the truth, even if it is hard to hear. Above all else, my clients know I care about them and the impact this work has on their life, not just their business.

Enough about me. Let me introduce you to two of the leaders who I have worked with, Rob and Jan. They both built "unicorns," privately held companies with a value of more than $1 billion, with my help. An infinitesimally small number of startups get to a billion-dollar valuation.

THE FOUNDER

In 2013 I was introduced to Rob Small. Rob was the co-founder and CEO of Miniclip, a gaming company based in London. With a focus on their website and the world moving to mobile, the business wasn't growing, and the management team who had gotten them this far wasn't equipped to take the business forward. The business was not in a great place, and Rob was asking tough questions of his own leadership.

However, we got to work; we strengthened the leadership team and developed a focused strategy committed to building a mobile gaming business. By 2015, Miniclip had come to the attention of Tencent, the Chinese technology and entertainment conglomerate, who acquired the business for a substantial undisclosed fee.

Ten years later, the business is 17.5X revenue and 13X users. Miniclip is now itself acquiring gaming businesses and growing apace. It is on the road to becoming a billion-dollar revenue company with one hundred million daily active users. Rob is the president and sits on the board. The current CEO, Saad Choudri, was promoted from within. I supported Rob throughout that journey, and I'm still supporting Miniclip today. Rob told me, "The contribution that you have made had a direct impact on the success of our business, Simon. It's been invaluable."

THE CORPORATE LEADER

Jan Bolz was in a senior international marketing role in Electronic Arts when I met him in 2005, and at that time, he was pretty skeptical about the value of coaching. Today, he's an investor and an evangelist for coaching. Jan's big opportunity came in 2011 when he was recruited as CEO of Tipico, the German sportsbook business. At that point, Tipico had no formal governance, little management, and a weak brand and cultural identity. The four founders had built the foundations for a successful business. However, they recognized that their "superpower" was not running the company, and they needed to appoint someone with the skills and temperament to do the CEO job well. That enabled them to focus on their areas of expertise.

The heart of our work together was building a strong, capable executive team, united around a clear strategy. Major investments in organization, people, and technology created huge growth in online and mobile. Working hard on himself and his team, Jan adapted well to the founder world, and by 2016, he and his team had transformed Tipico into a unicorn. CVC Capital Partners acquired a majority stake based on a valuation well in excess of €1 billion. Jan told me, "I am happy to admit, Simon, that we never would have achieved this without your support and constant hard work with the leadership group." Jan left Tipico in 2016, and the shareholders appointed Jochen Baca as CEO. Jochen's deep experience of the industry powered Tipico to new levels of excellence and performance.

———

Rob adapted to the demands of the leadership role and became an outstanding founder CEO. Jan adapted to the demands of the founder environment and became an excellent CEO, too. Both Rob and Jan had the right mindset and did the hard work. They were driven by a sense of purpose and conviction, not simply financial outcomes.

These stories of billion-dollar success are both dramatic and rare. Miniclip and Tipico are now strong, sustainable businesses with many employees. And although the underlying ingredients for that success were recognizably in place (a large, addressable market, technology that works at scale, the right timing, and a clear path to profitability), it's the leadership and the team they've built around them that is most pivotal.

BUILDING A GREAT BUSINESS

Founding a business means you or your co-founder will likely become its first CEO—but having the game-changing idea and building the business are two very different things. You will need to embrace the fact that you are in a leadership role, whether you like it or not, and approach it with a combination of courage and humility. Adopting this mindset will help you to face the challenges ahead.

What do I mean by building a *great* business? Financial markets and investors would traditionally place a premium on businesses that deliver sustainable growth in earnings. From this perspective, *all* decisions should be weighed by their impact on financial returns. *Great* companies, however, view profit not as the sole end, but as a way of ensuring returns will continue and the business is sustainable. At their heart they have a purpose and seek to produce products or services that improve users' lives, provide jobs, and enhance their workers' quality of life. We live in an age when leaders and companies are closely scrutinized, and consumers and employees have the power and choice to seek tangible value. The firm is a social institution, not just an economic one. This definition of a great company is at the heart of the challenge facing founders today: building a strong, purposeful, and valuable business that will stand the test of time.

Given this demanding context and the challenges involved in building a great business, founders should be admired for their courage. They are trying to build something special and are prepared to take a risk and back themselves. One of my biggest motivations for writing this book is to help people who demonstrate such courage.

ADOPTING A GROWTH MINDSET

In 2014, *Harvard Business Review* reported that founders of enterprises valued at $1 billion or more by venture capitalists tend to cluster in the twenty to thirty-four age range. Younger leaders are likely to be rich in what Arthur C. Brooks, in his book *From Strength to Strength*, calls "fluid intelligence."[1] Fluid intelligence is the capacity to think speedily and reason flexibly in order to solve new problems without relying on past experience and accumulated knowledge. It peaks relatively early in adulthood and diminishes in one's thirties and forties. Founders will lean heavily on this capability as they start to build and grow their businesses. Innovators typically have an abundance of fluid intelligence.

As I have passed sixty years, my fluid intelligence has definitely peaked (that's life!), and founders and leaders my age rely more on our "crystalized intelligence"—the ability to utilize skills and knowledge acquired via prior learning, recalling of preexisting information, as well as skills. Because crystalized intelligence relies on an accumulating stock of knowledge, it tends to increase through one's forties and does not diminish until very late in life. Crystalized intelligence means using your experience to know the right questions, even if the answers come less easily. No one knows all the answers. But with my considerable breadth and depth of experience as a leadership coach and a founder leader, I do ask thoughtful questions. Great questions force us to think and find our own answers. As Ray Dalio says in his book *Principles*, "Smart people are the ones who ask the most thoughtful questions, as opposed to thinking they have all the answers. Great questions are a much better indicator of future success than great answers."[2]

Every founder recognizes that original thinking is pivotal to the success of their business idea—and the same is true of how they build the business itself. The world of a founder does not work in a linear, sequential, or controllable way, and there's no universal formula for success. (That's why this book is *not* called something like *Eight Rules for Excellence!*) You need to find your own answers.

However (just to contradict myself a little), there is perhaps one golden rule that I have seen in action time and again: "Work harder on yourself than you do on your job," as said by American entrepreneur, author, and speaker Jim Rohn. Like profit, best pursued by strengthening the drivers of profit (such as a great customer experience or a smart strategy), the more you work on your own development, the more successful you will be in achieving your business goals. How do you do that when you are flat-out busy? Together we will explore the answer, one page at a time. But the starting point is to bring a growth mindset. Carol Dweck from Stanford University first coined the term *growth mindset* in her book *Mindset: The New Psychology of Success*. She says, "The hallmark of successful people is that they are always stretching themselves to learn new things."[3] In *Bounce*, Matthew Syed argues that it is intensive training, not natural ability, that determines our success, and people who attribute great performances to natural gifts will probably miss their own chance to succeed due to lack of practice.[4]

HOW TO USE THIS BOOK

So, you need to find your own answers, and you need to practice. This book will challenge you to do both in order to bring a growth mindset to both you and your venture.

It is worth reading the entire book from front to back, cover to cover. As a guide, I would suggest setting aside a minimum of ten minutes per day to read and reflect on a single part that contains stories, lessons from experience, relevant research, questions, and practical suggestions for you to work through. Once you have absorbed the core concepts, you can thumb through the pages as needed, choosing the sections most relevant to your current challenges and ambitions.

The first part of this book considers what it takes to lead successfully. When people see your apparent success, they don't typically see your self-doubt, variable motivation, many failures, and sleepless nights. We explore your strengths as a leader, what you stand for, and how you can show up at your best. We discuss practical ways to manage your energy and build resilience to face the inevitable difficulties of founding and growing a business and prepare you for the choices that lie ahead, including how your role and involvement may change over time. This part of the book enables you to figure out who you are and how you want to be as a leader. Emotional energy is gained when we understand ourselves. We feel freer to choose—and we make better choices, too.

The second part is about getting your venture in shape to deliver on its purpose. We consider the job of a CEO and the four powerful dimensions of leadership that you should seek to master. We orientate where your business is today, the journey that lies ahead, and what that entails. And we explore the leadership fundamentals facing you: purpose, strategy, organization, culture, and talent. By the end, you will have a strong sense of where your business is in good shape, where you have work to do, and how to think about and approach that work. You will have grasped the essence of the leadership job that you face.

The third part of this book supports you to master the myriad of tactical challenges you will typically face as a CEO: setting goals, motivating people, hiring, building teams, making tough decisions, and many more. Each chapter explores an area I have helped CEOs with a growth mindset to work on multiple times. Each should help you to feel more resourceful and confident to tackle that challenge thoughtfully, in your own unique context. I encourage you to take author Marie Forleo's advice to heart: "Clarity comes from engagement, not thought!"[5] In other words, act now, and you will find your truth. All of us, without exception, learn from practice, whether you are trying to set strategy or behave more empathetically. The questions in this book are not there just to make you think; they're there to give you the confidence to *act*.

BEING PURPOSE-LED

Before we start, if your philosophy is to view the people in your business as assets and your central preoccupation is with money, this book will probably annoy you at times! In my experience, sustainable financial performance comes from finding people who share your purpose and contribute to creating a successful strategy and business model—and then finding ways to help them to do amazing work.

We are all faced with a less-than-benign world, and we're becoming used to shocks, such as the pandemic, that are hard to foresee. Navigating this world requires more than business acumen and a desire for returns. It requires a sense of purpose and values to guide your venture through these choppy waters.

So, if you think that becoming a successful founder is only about creating a winning product that meets a customer need, you are in for a shock. You will need to navigate these rough seas, and your business will face significant public scrutiny as it does so. My guess is that you already see this; many of the founders I meet and work with are purpose-driven people with strong values who don't just focus on wealth creation.

These founders also know full well that many consumers are similarly values driven. Most of the things we use do not get reused. Climate change is accelerating, and we are continuing to destroy the biodiversity of our planet. This destruction impacts food security, public health, poverty, and inequality. More and more founders are realizing the power of business to impact positive change—not only to be resilient in the face of the volatility we are all experiencing.

What does a company that is fit for the present and the future look like? In their book, *Net Positive*, former CEO of Unilever Paul Polman and sustainability expert Andrew Winston describe such a company as—

> Taking responsibility for the company's impacts on the wider world
> Focusing more on the long term (while seeking good results in all time frames)
> Serving multiple stakeholders and putting their needs first
> Embracing collaboration and transformative change beyond the company
> Providing shareholders with solid returns[6]

The evidence suggests that such companies deliver higher returns for shareholders, not lower. Why? Because they are more resilient, they attract the best talent, and their employees are more motivated.

Businesses cannot thrive in societies that fail. A *net positive* business profits from solving the world's problems, not creating them. Is the world better off because your business is in it? Polman argues that putting yourself at the service of others will ultimately be to your benefit as well.[7]

Society needs purpose-driven founders and leaders who want to change the world for the better—leaders who are human first, care about their children's future, and want a healthier, safer, and more just world.

Whatever your goals, becoming a founder and leader will certainly change you.

PART I

WHAT IT TAKES TO LEAD

CHAPTER 1

Working on Yourself

Love challenges, be intrigued by mistakes, enjoy effort, and keep on learning.

—**Carol Dweck,** *Mindset*

The more you work on your own development, the more successful you will be in achieving your business goals. If you have taken the step to start your own business, you already are stepping out of your comfort zone and demonstrating courage. But that first step is only the beginning of your story as a founder and entrepreneur.

You are going to face many obstacles. At times, the context will help you—and at other times, it will make it extremely tough. Pandemics happen; businesses get shuttered. Wars are declared; inflation takes off. Your success cannot depend on things you cannot change; it must depend on what you *can* change. One thing you can change is you. You can grow more resilient, more informed, more skilled, and more effective at leading your business. And that is very good news because it is firmly within your grasp. Don't wish for less problems; make yourself stronger.

This is not a call to work harder. Most entrepreneurs work hard already. It is a warning to potential founders and entrepreneurs that you are going to need more "smarts" than that. You will certainly need hard work, grit, and a readiness to be uncomfortable if you want to build a successful business. Founders often face a genuine struggle to get their business off the ground. There will be difficult conversations persuading others to invest or believe in you. You will have to repeatedly put yourself in situations where you feel out of your depth. You will be disappointed by people on whom you thought you could rely. You will take risks that do not pay off.

I could continue, but I don't want to put you off completely! You are never, ever the finished article. You will be tested in ways you cannot imagine. You will experience failure. And the successful are those who learn from those experiences rather than feel defeated by them. Learning to lead is about personal growth and becoming the most valuable version of yourself you can be. If you work on yourself, you can build an extremely valuable business. If you don't, you are left with hope, luck, and grind. It will exhaust you.

Treating yourself as "the finished article" is what some have called a fixed mindset. You are at risk from being derailed by any event or problem you simply do not know how to solve. A life of experience, and not just in business, tells me that you need a growth mindset, a belief that you can and must develop your skills and talents. This requires a combination of disciplined learning, self-evaluation, and the ability to learn from mistakes.

With the right motivation, realistic self-insight, and intentional practice of new behaviors, personal growth becomes second nature. It will enable you to transform your business. And this hunger to learn and grow should never stop. It's not only for the inexperienced but also for everyone throughout their careers.

So, what can you do to practice working from a growth mindset?

> Start with the view that your abilities can be developed through dedication and hard work—there is nothing "fixed" about you!

> Why do you want to improve? Get clear about what's in it for you.

> Practice, practice, practice. Do the work. Keep stretching yourself. And seek feedback without fear or favor from everyone who sees your practice.

> Grasp every opportunity you get to take steps forward: a chance to speak at a conference; coaching from someone you respect.

In my introduction, you met Jan Bolz, who later went on to become the CEO of Tipico. When I first met Jan at EA, he was in a difficult situation and receiving criticism about his performance. Jan initially saw the offer of coaching as an imposition; in his mind, the problems lay elsewhere. At that stage, he thought he had little to learn. This fixed mindset sees the need to learn as a direct challenge to the ego. Jan was looking for opportunities to show me that he already knew all the answers. But in the safe space of a coaching relationship, he began to open up. He became much more honest with both himself and me. He realized that whatever else is going on, nothing stops you from working on yourself. In fact, if you want to change something, the first thing you have to do is work on yourself.

At one point, Jan was asked to speak at his company's international conference. He is German, not a natural communicator in English, and felt uncomfortable presenting. However, he was highly motivated to share his vision at the conference, and he worked hard to refine what he wanted to share. I helped him to "anglicize" his storyboard and impact. He practiced until he knew the content by heart. He got feedback from people he trusted and practiced some more, and he focused on his delivery.

Finally, the day of the conference arrived, and Jan was nervous. I was in the audience, sitting next to someone who knew him. It was obvious that this person expected the presentation to be a train wreck. What he saw shocked him—a natural, compelling performance. Jan went on to become a hugely successful CEO, not because of his presentation skills— but because of the remarkable growth mindset that powered his personal development, and still does.

Jan, Rob Small, the president of Miniclip, and many other leaders I have coached are successful not *because* they have never struggled; they are successful because they learned from failure. We need to fail to learn how to succeed. As a leader, whatever the context, you know you are responsible. So, if something isn't right, it's your responsibility to change it . . . starting with yourself.

Reflections on Working on Yourself

1. What talents do you already possess? What strengths do the success of your venture depend on and which do you need to continue to practice?

2. What do you need to learn to take your venture to the next level?

3. Where and how can you practice the skills you need to develop?

4. Who can you surround yourself with to help you see yourself accurately and to guide you? Do you need a mentor or a coach?

5. How can you ensure that every success or failure you experience is grasped as an opportunity for learning and growth?

CHAPTER 2

Not Being Alone

A startup is too much work for one person.

—Paul Graham, co-founder of Y Combinator[1]

As Elon Musk said, "A company is a group of people that are organized to create a product or service. That's what a company is."[2] The most important thing, he goes on to say, is to "attract great people."[3] Warren Buffett adds that we should surround ourselves with people who are better than us, those who will help us to find the best pathway.[4]

That starts from the very beginning of your story. Are you thinking of setting up on your own or have you joined forces with a co-founder?

There is a widely held view among many, including venture capitalists, that new ventures perform better when launched by teams rather than individuals. There is data to back that up. Ali Tamaseb, partner at DCVC and author of *Super Founders*, found that having two or three co-founders is the ideal scenario if you are trying to build a unicorn. However, it is worth noting that 20 percent of all billion-dollar startups since 2005 had a solo founder. And Jeff Bezos has done OK.

Research published in 2018 by Jason Greenberg and Ethan Mollick of Wharton showed that companies started by solo founders actually survive *longer* than those started by teams.[5] A *Harvard Business Review* article revealed that solo founders are not actually solo at all.[6] They have what the authors call "co-creators" who aren't official co-founders but still play a critical role in helping founders build their businesses (without forcing them to give up equity or risk co-founder drama). These co-creators might be employees, alliances, or benefactors.

Overall, the evidence suggests that teams *do* outperform individuals, but that doesn't mean the team has to be made up of co-founders. The game changer with a brilliant idea needs somebody who gets things done. The salesperson needs the coder and vice versa. Daniel Ek and Martin Lorentzon established Spotify AB in Sweden in 2006, with Ek as CEO and Lorentzon as chairman. Between them, they knew what it would take to build Spotify into the company it is today. As a business grows, it rapidly needs to consider who else is needed to take the business forward. Andreas Ehn immediately became Spotify's first employee and CTO. Andreas, in turn, was responsible for the product and platform architecture, as well as hiring a world-class engineering team.

The winning team may be different from the founding team. Mark Zuckerberg had co-founders at Facebook. But eventually they drifted off, and the real turning point for the company was hiring a non-founder, Sheryl Sandberg, who had the skill set that Mark didn't have. Arguably, that was the moment that turbocharged the company. Facebook isn't a success today because Zuckerberg had co-founders—it's a success because he made good hires.

Perhaps the best strategy for startups is to do everything possible to find the *right* co-founder at the outset. Co-founders of Limbic AI, a mental health chatbot tool, Sebastiaan (Bas) de Vries and Dr. Ross Harper met through Entrepreneur First (EF). EF selects individuals they recognize as having huge founder potential and brings them together to build globally ambitious technology companies at a rapid pace. Bas, the CTO, told me (with a grin) that when he met his co-founder Ross (now the CEO), it was "love at first sight." What he meant was that he loved the way Ross's brain worked, the way he thought, and the way he made decisions. He also admired how Ross communicated, something Bas was less good at, which ultimately led to the mutual decision that Ross should be CEO. Although EF was nudging Bas and Ross to consider alternative co-founders (neither had a commercial focus; they both were tech-savvy), their business has gone from strength to strength. And they have now appointed a strong commercial leader for their business.

The sooner the founder(s) realize they cannot do it all themselves and need to build the right team around them, the sooner the business starts to flourish. One of the classic errors is trying to do it all yourself, or to be more precise, not recognizing when to let go and appoint people better than yourself or with a greater specialist skill.

Much depends on what kind of person you are, which is why there is a chapter of this book dedicated to that topic. Take me—I am a natural Play Maker. So, for me, the most natural thing to do when I started to form my own business was to gather smart people whom I trusted. A good move, but my naivete was exposed when I asked the group, "What is *our* vision?" Nickie, a smart woman who has been one of my mentors for many years, said, "Simon, we are all here because we believe in you. It's not *our* vision that we are interested in; it's yours." My first lesson in being the founder CEO—show up, be accountable, and be clear about your vision.

Other founders have the opposite struggle: an unwillingness to share, listen, or involve others. That will lead to failure, too. Our natural proclivities are both the strengths that enable us to succeed and, when overused, the seeds of our own downfall. This is yet more evidence of the need for a growth mindset. I felt embarrassed by my first misstep in a leadership role. But I had the sense to listen, learn, and adapt based on the feedback I received—and keep that level of support and challenge around me for the whole life of my tenure as CEO and beyond.

As a coach, I have observed that many, even most, founders are quite lonely. One reason for this is that founder CEOs in particular do not want to look vulnerable, weak, or uncertain, so they don't share what is troubling them. They want to maintain the confidence of their investors and team, even a co-founder. Generally speaking, this is not smart and probably suggests that they have not forged the right relationships with the right people. But if that *is* the reality, a coach can be a lifeline.

I encourage founders, when they are feeling stressed about a choice they have to make, to talk to their team about it wherever possible. In my experience, nothing bad has ever happened from asking the team to weigh in on founder-level decisions. It brings the team closer together, makes everyone more invested in the business, and, on a personal level, makes a founder feel less isolated.

Often founders come to me with this problem: "Everything is flying at me, and I don't know what is important." This leads to stress and health issues, so it needs an outlet and some strategies for dealing with it. Some kind of triage system can help—focusing on the real priorities and letting go of things that are less important or that can be asked of others. Another big area is relationship problems—facing up to the need for and preparing for challenging conversations with investors, board members, or the team. The health and breakout success of a growing company can be unlocked or blocked by the health of its CEO and their team. Solo founder or not, do not try to go it alone.

The English word *company* has its origins in the old French term *compagnie* (first recorded in 1150), meaning a "society, friendship, intimacy; body of soldiers," which came from the Latin word *companio* ("one who eats bread with you").

Reflections on Not Being Alone

1. If you have a co-founder, do you have the right person and relationship to succeed?

2. Do you have the right people around you—people with the right competence who both support and/or challenge you?

3. Do you have someone around you with whom you can share your personal and business development challenges?

4. If the answer to any of the first three questions is no, what are you going to do about it?

CHAPTER 3

Managing Your Energy

Efficiency is concerned with doing things right. Effectiveness is doing the right things.

—Peter Drucker, consultant and author

Time is a finite resource, so it should be treated as a precious commodity. It's not to be wasted—especially for a founder with many demands to navigate. Peter Drucker also said, "There is surely nothing quite so useless as doing with great efficiency what should not be done at all."[1]

Entrepreneurs typically are driven people. When they launch a business, they tend to work long hours, driven both by their sense of purpose and by their fear of failure. The latter is frequently the most powerful driver in my experience. This is understandable, and pulling long hours may be unavoidable for certain periods such as the buildup to a product launch or during fundraising. But none of us are indestructible; we are all human. Sustained long hours are ultimately unsustainable, like trying to run a marathon at a pace your body simply cannot cope with. And this leads to poor performance even if it creates the illusion of productivity in the short run.

In a 2007 *Harvard Business Review* article, Tony Schwartz and Catherine McCarthy highlight that although time is a finite resource, energy is a different story. Energy comes from four main sources in human beings: the body, emotions, mind, and spirit. In each, energy can be systematically expanded and regularly renewed by establishing specific habits—behaviors that are intentionally practiced, with the goal of making them unconscious and automatic as quickly as possible.[2]

Many founders work long hours and neglect themselves. Perhaps you are doing this? To recharge, you need to recognize the cost of energy-depleting behaviors and then take responsibility for changing them, regardless of the circumstances you're facing. Schwartz and McCarthy provide a helpful audit that includes specific behaviors linked to all four sources of energy. For example, the body needs sufficient sleep, good nutrition, exercise, and breaks from work.

Doing this kind of self-audit is helpful because it can reveal where the issues and opportunities lie. We typically underestimate the importance of sufficient, good quality sleep, for instance. In his book *Lost Connections*, Johann Hari highlights that the average person sleeps about an hour less than in 1942 (that's 20 percent less). Only 15 percent of us awake feeling refreshed.[3] This has big implications for our attention and ability to think. Sleep is the time when our body is repaired.

Johann's book is an important contribution to our understanding of what makes it hard for us to focus during our work time. The average time we are able to focus on one task is apparently a mere three minutes. Our inability to focus has significant costs. It leads to mistakes, memory loss, and lost time to recover where the mind was before the interruption. One of the biggest stealers of our attention is that small but powerful computer that's probably at arm's length from you right now. Manage it.

So, we need to be both mindful, and intentional, about how we protect our focus and use our time. Because focus compounds faster than money.

Rick Ross writes about how to create time in Peter Senge's book *The Dance of Change*. In it, he provides some practical ideas for creating time, which many of my coaching clients have found valuable and which still resonate with me. I summarize them for you here:[4]

1. *Prune your change initiatives.*

   Look at all the things you are doing: It may be all "good stuff," but chances are, there's too much of it. Use this payoff matrix to evaluate organizational improvement suggestions and focus on the two or three highest-leverage efforts:

	Easy to accomplish	Difficult to accomplish
High impact on the organization	1	2
Low impact on the organization	3	4

2. *Choose decision styles that don't waste time.*

   Be clear about who's making the decision and how. Being clear will save a lot of wasted time. Is it telling, selling, testing, consulting, or co-creating? Bryan Smith originally developed this framework, detailed in *The Fifth Discipline Fieldbook.*[5]

3. *Check your calendar against your vision.*

   Look at the appointments you have made for the next couple of months against the demands of the vision for your company, team, and self. How much of this time is "non-aligned" and therefore nonessential? What can you stop doing?

4. *Do an attention appraisal.*

   Ask your team members to list things that you pay too much attention to and things that you don't pay enough attention to. Ask them to be candid and then act on the feedback.

5. *Reduce your oversight.*

What tasks do you wish you didn't have to bother doing that you could delegate to someone else? What tasks shouldn't you be doing? What tasks could you handle with a lot less oversight? For example, what level of expenses do you really need to approve?

I find number three, check your calendar against your vision, particularly powerful. And you can apply it retrospectively, not just to assess your upcoming schedule. Most CEOs I coach find that they are way off—in other words, their vision and time choices are significantly misaligned. This creates a big opportunity. Never say, "I don't have the time." Your time use reflects your priorities and your values. If you care enough about something, you will create the time to do it. Doing an audit of where your time is going reveals the reality and enables you to start to make intentional choices that maximize the value contribution of your time. Be laser-focused on your priorities. Invest your energy where you will get the best returns and make sure you replenish that energy loss.

I suspect the truth is that many founders love what they do and want to do it, even deep into the evenings or weekends. If they are pursuing their purpose and enjoying their work, why would they switch off? Even if this is true for you, you still have to manage your energy. Find the right rhythm for yourself so you translate what energizes you into good habits and a consistent pattern of time use.

In an article published on the *BetterUp Blog*, Shonna Waters describes how a number of famous leaders manage their energy, not their time.[6] Warren Buffett, for example, schedules days in his calendar when he has nothing specific to do. He wants to protect that time to think rather than to do. Jeff Bezos sets his first meetings no earlier than 10:00 a.m. because he values the time he has with his family in the morning. Fashion designer and founder CEO Anine Bing starts her day with meditation, taking the time to be still and intentional with her thoughts. Her meditation practice gives her the energy she needs and helps her remain present in her other tasks. Consider scheduling time for deeper work, exercise, rest and recovery, and your family. Don't allow these activities to be completely "squeezed out" by busy work. Avoid micromanagement and learn to delegate.

Being a founder is tough. You need to take care of yourself. When I meet a leader to coach them (face-to-face or online), I can usually see at a glance whether they are in the performance zone or at risk of burnout. It is that obvious. When tired people combine with tricky business challenges, it's hard to think straight and act smart. Don't make the mistake of postponing a healthy life while you pull long hours. A healthy life is what will help you to perform at your best as a leader, and it's what will build a high-performing business.

Reflections on Managing Your Energy

1. Are you managing your energy with some care and intention? Are you changing energy-depleting behaviors so you show up in the best shape?

2. What are you spending your time on and is it the most productive choice? What does the business really need from you right now?

3. How are you protecting your focus so that when you need to, you can work at your best?

4. How can you translate your vision and priorities into a daily, weekly, and monthly rhythm that enables you to lead well and take care of your health, too?

CHAPTER 4

Building Diverse Relationships

Invest in great relationships, they will pay a lifetime of dividends.

—Bill Walsh, American football coach

In chapter 2, we talked about not being alone. Building on that, I want to talk about the value of your network and how to make it count. Some people just get it and do it instinctively. Extroverts develop their ideas through engaging with others—they are energized and informed by it. But despite this, leaders of all personality types frequently don't invest the time or the energy to network wisely. Why does this matter? And what can you do about it?

From the very beginning of your life as a founder, you will have benefited from the people you know and the relationships you build. They might give you access to clients, talent, or funding. When I started building my own business, I relied extensively on referrals, and I still benefit from them today. All the best people I work with as fellow coaches and consultants came through personal, trusted introductions. In three cases, a client became a partner in our practice some years later—what better demonstration of the value of trusted relationships?

Depending on the stage of development of your business, you will have different network priorities. For example, in the early stages, you may be most interested to talk to people in your target customer group. In my experience, people will be interested to talk to you if you have something to offer them, not simply because you want something from them. Develop your network around your idea. Show curiosity and go out of your way to help them. If you behave authentically, you won't feel "dirty" doing it. Many of us feel uncomfortable about networking if we are honest with ourselves. Tap into that growth mindset, and you will overcome the reticence.

As you try to establish your business brand, showing up and speaking at events is a great way to position your business and the values and ideas you are trying to promote. We've found this is a vital way to bring clients and potential clients together, and a way to help others to broaden their thinking and their network.

Roselinde Torres, who leads Boston Consulting Group's CEO advisory practice in North America, uses her platform to ask us to consider the diversity measure of our personal and professional networks.[1] In the digital age, ideas tend to come from anywhere, and the most successful ideas come from connecting diverse networks of people from various disciplines. Studies show that more diversity in your network makes it easier to spot patterns, innovate, and create a positive impact. Be honest: Where does your ability lie in building relationships with people who are very different from you? Do you network with people at the intersections of multiple disciplines? Can you ask profound, thoughtful questions to promote innovative solutions to old and new problems? Diverse networks create new ways of thinking and game-changing ideas.

We explore this idea further in chapter 38 on building diverse teams. They take time to build, but the investment pays off if you are patient and put in the work.

Another insight that points us toward a wider network is a fifty-year-old study by one of the pioneers of social network theory. In 1973, Stanford sociology professor Mark Granovetter published an empirical paper called "The Strength of Weak Ties." It became one of the most influential sociology papers of all time. In social networks, you have different links—or ties—to other people. Strong ties are characterized as deep affinity—for example, family, friends, or colleagues. Weak ties, in contrast, might be acquaintances, or strangers with a common cultural background. The point is that the strength of these ties can substantially affect interactions, outcomes, and well-being.[2]

Granovetter's work showed that much of our *new* information comes from weak ties. He "surveyed 282 Boston-based workers and found that most of them got their jobs through someone they knew. But only a minority got the job through a close friend; 84 percent got their job through those weak-tie relationships—meaning casual contacts they saw only occasionally. As Granovetter pointed out, the people with whom you spend a lot of time swim in the same pool of information as you do."[3] We depend on friendly outsiders to bring us news of opportunities beyond our immediate circles—and the more of those acquaintances we have, the better.

On a personal level, I have experienced a huge benefit from someone who was originally a "weak tie." I had worked with Rachel Page in a previous company some years before. Out of the blue, she called me to ask if I knew someone who offered training in a particular area. I was able to help her, and while on the call, we chatted about what we were both doing. She was working for an American video game company and was looking for a coach for a UK-based leader. That conversation led to a series of projects and a whole sequence of client relationships and work in the industry. It also created some lifetime friendships.

This exploitation of weak ties can be scaled up. For example, many Silicon Valley tech companies are currently prototypical tight networks of white male engineers educated at Stanford or MIT. Many of these companies have abysmal diversity numbers. Contrast this with a company whose founding team is diverse. Such a team will have both strong and weak ties that bridge to many different networks of underrepresented engineers, designers, and managers. This diversity will continue to grow because these new employees also bridge to many different networks of talented people. These teams have a compounding advantage in credibility and reach that makes it hard for non-diverse teams to catch up in a highly competitive marketplace for talent.

Reflections on Building Diverse Relationships

1. Are you mindful of the power of a network and ready to invest time and energy in it to support your growth and the growth of your business?

2. What is the diversity measure of your network? Are you spending enough time with people from very different backgrounds than yours?

3. Do you spend your time exclusively with your strong ties? What can you do to reach out to and stay more connected with your weak ties?

CHAPTER 5

Identifying Your Default Patterns

To understand is to perceive patterns.

—Isaiah Berlin, philosopher

W ho are you, really? What are your strengths? Whatever they are, they will be the key to your success, so capitalize on them. What are your weaknesses? Whatever they are, you need to surround yourself with people who compensate for them. Without self-awareness, you can do neither. It is one of the key ingredients required for personal growth.

In his classic 1998 book about emotional intelligence, Daniel Goleman pioneered the idea that "the ability to recognize and understand your moods, emotions, and drives, as well as their effect on others" was a hallmark of effective leaders.[1]

This matters to the business, not just to you. Korn Ferry tracked the stock performance of nearly five hundred public companies over thirty months, between 2010 and 2013. They searched a total of nearly seven thousand self-assessments from professionals at these companies to iden-tify the "blind spots" in individuals' leadership characteristics. During that period the companies with the greater percentage of self-aware employees consistently outperformed those with a lower percentage.[2]

Founder of hedge fund Bridgewater Associates Ray Dalio has written about the importance of understanding how people are wired in his book *Principles*. He argues that because of the different ways our brains are wired, we all experience reality in different ways, and any single way is essentially distorted. So, if you want to know what is true and what to do about it, you must understand your own brain. How are you wired? It's not so easy to answer that question, and we often struggle to find the right language to do it. And our self-insight varies enormously—how we are and how we prefer to see ourselves are sometimes a bit different.

So, if understanding ourselves is so important to our growth as a leader, how can we gain that deeper understanding? There are a variety of ways:

> *Trusted feedback*—Feedback leads to empathy and helps you under-stand the impact of your actions on others.

> *Journaling*—Practice regular self-reflection about patterns in your behaviors, assessing those patterns in light of external triggers and what drives you, including your values and priorities.

> *Coaching*—With an experienced coach, tease out the patterns of behavior you demonstrate and what triggers them, and learn how to see yourself in context.

> *Testing*—With the support of a trained interpreter, use psychomet-ric testing or something similar to explore patterns of personality and behavior.

I frequently use a profiling tool called The GC Index® that is extremely beneficial in helping people to understand and act on their natural pro-clivities. It has the additional value, when used in a team context, of recognizing the contributions and impact that each person has on the success of the team. Research shows it takes months for team members to learn how to get the best out of one another. This instrument reduces that to hours.

There are many tools available in the market, mostly psychometrics, that help us to understand our personality. The value of The GC Index® is that it focuses on behavior, an individual's "energy for impact," and the effect this can have on the team and the business. I want to maximize the impact and contribution my clients can make to the organization so they feel individually and collectively *potent*. As Dr. John Mervyn-Smith, one of the co-creators of The GC Index®, puts it, "Human beings are 'hard-wired' to have an impact upon their world; the basis for surviving and thriving. The GC Index profiles the ways in which individuals and groups seek to channel their energy when it comes to making that impact."[3]

Research behind The GC Index® shows that people differ when it comes to their proclivities for making a positive *impact* on their world. These differences are underpinned by an individual's

> Capacity for original thought—*Imagination*

> Drive to turn ideas into reality—*Obsession*

The five GC Index® proclivities are described in Figure 5.1.

Many business founders are Game Changers, though not all, by any means. When we looked at a population of 271 business owners, we noted that 57 percent of that group had Game Changer as one of their two highest proclivities, and 34 percent had Strategist as one of their two highest. The data for a population of company directors in established businesses flipped these numbers around. Both Game Changers and Strategists have energy for making an impact with ideas, but their focus will be different, and this will be evident as leaders of businesses. Strategists as business leaders are typically derivative with their thinking (they build upon the patterns and trends they see within their world), purposeful, planned, and pragmatic.

The GC Index® Five Proclivities

STRATEGIST
MAPS
THE FUTURE

These individuals see the future. They engage others with clear direction that brings focus to action.

GAME CHANGER
TRANSFORMS
THE FUTURE

These are the individuals who generate the ideas and possibilities that have the potential to be transformative.

PLAY MAKER
ORCHESTRATES
THE FUTURE

These are the individuals who focus on getting the best from others individually and collectively, in support of agreed objectives.

IMPLEMENTER
BUILDS
THE FUTURE

These are the individuals who get things done. As leaders they shape strategic plans and deliver tangible outcomes.

POLISHER
CREATES A FUTURE
TO BE PROUD OF

These individuals create a future to be proud of. They focus on making things better, continual improvement, and the pursuit of excellence.

Figure 5.1. Image by permission of The GC Index®. All rights reserved.

36

Game Changers at their best see possibilities others often don't. They are not constrained by what has gone before. Game Changers as business leaders are typically original, obsessed with their ideas, and opportunistic. Their drive and creativity come with a single-minded nature—this may mean they are not seen as patient or open to influence, and this will distort relationships for some. This combination of drive, creativity, and single-mindedness is what gives a new venture liftoff. It can also lead to problems once the team grows and scaling becomes the priority—which is why teams are so important in the story of a founder (see chapter 38).

As a coach, I don't try to *fix* someone; I try to *see* them and then help them to perform better in a way that is authentic. I cannot—and have no intention of—rewiring their brain, as Ray Dalio would put it, but I can help them understand their own default patterns. In that way, they can become the best version of themselves, a more defined and refined version, if you like. As I said in chapter 2, our natural proclivities are both the strengths that enable us to succeed and, when overused, the seeds of our own downfall.

For example, I am coaching someone who is driven, direct, and an excellent problem-solver. At his best, he is straightforward to deal with and really good at cutting through complex problems. With that, he can be insensitive and too ready to solve the problem himself, unintentionally stripping ownership and learning away from team members. It's not only important to understand an overused strength, but also to understand times where your strengths could produce negative results based on the situation. In this case, my client is so results-oriented that he becomes overcontrolling and does not take people with him, which is quite demotivating. He is learning to be much more mindful of the people he is working with and how to get the best out of them—not just a problem-solver but also a problem-solver coach. He is now teaching his team members to become better problem-solvers.

Reflections on Identifying Your Default Patterns

1. How might you strengthen your self-insight?

2. What help do you need from others to truly understand yourself and how are you going to secure that help?

3. How can you use that insight to become a more effective leader?

CHAPTER 6

Finding Your Purpose

The two most important days in your life are the day you are born and the day you find out why.

—Mark Twain

What is your purpose? This is an ancient question. But it has particular resonance in the world we live in today, given the pace of change and the ease with which we can feel rudderless, pulled in many directions at once. And it's easy to mistake goals for purpose. In a business setting, profit is a result, not a purpose. Equally, becoming rich, for example, is *not* a purpose.

So, given that, what is a purpose, and how does that link to your growth and effectiveness as a leader? One of the roles of a leader is to provide a purpose and create a culture that gives meaning and a beating heart to your organization. You won't be able to do that unless *you* have a deep sense of that purpose.

When starting a business, the majority of people and companies start with "what"—the product. Simon Sinek asks us to start with the motivation: your purpose. Because, as he puts it in his book *Start with Why*, inspired leaders communicate from the inside out.

Why does purpose matter? Research shows that people who score high on purpose are grittier than those who are pleasure-oriented (focused on their own interest). In *Grit: The Power of Passion and Perseverance*, Angela Duckworth explains why purpose is what drives perseverance, which carries you through the tough times. Duckworth says, "When I talk to people about their work, and they tell me that it's meaningful or it has purpose . . . they always end up telling a story about how it's part of something bigger than themselves, and it improves other people's lives."[1]

What impact are you trying to have? What do you want your legacy to be? These are the questions that will power your leadership conviction.

Answering these questions will also keep you in good health. Alan Rozanski, a professor at the Icahn School of Medicine at Mount Sinai, has studied the relationship between life purpose and physical health. "Just like people have basic physical needs, like to sleep and eat and drink, they have basic psychological needs," he says. "The need for meaning and purpose is No. 1," Rozanski adds. "It's the deepest driver of well-being there is."[2] Research seems to back this up.

One study carried out in the United States found that people who didn't have a strong life purpose—defined as "a self-organizing life aim that stimulates goals"—were more likely to die than those who did, and specifically more likely to die of cardiovascular diseases. People without a strong life purpose were more than twice as likely to die between the study years of 2006 and 2010, compared with those who had one. Having a life purpose appeared to be more important for decreasing risk of death than drinking, smoking, or exercising regularly![3]

Purpose, then, is a powerful fuel. Purpose-driven leaders are happier, healthier, and more motivated. Purpose alignment is a principal motivator for *all of us*. Imagine a team or workforce that is fully purpose-aligned with you, showing high levels of grit, motivation, and health. We will explore how to create that later in the book.

So, what is *your* purpose? What gives your work meaning for you? If you can uncover it, it will empower you to power your business to success. This is a profound question that takes time and reflection to answer. It won't come to you without some intention.

Look back on your life so far. When did you feel happiest? Don't be distracted by fleeting experiences, such as when you were on holiday. When you're giving your fullest attention to an activity or task that you're incredibly passionate about, singularly focused on, and totally immersed in, you may find yourself creating the conditions necessary to experience a flow state of mind. The flow mental state is generally less common during periods of relaxation and makes itself present during challenging and engaging activities. According to Mihaly Csikszentmihalyi, author of *Flow*, "The best moments in our lives are not the passive, receptive, relaxing times . . . the best moments usually occur if a person's body or mind is stretched to its limits in a voluntary effort to accomplish something difficult and worthwhile."[4] To that end, engagement and concentration are key in achieving flow state. I have this feeling when I am fully engrossed in my coaching work.

Try to put aside others' expectations of you. Focus on your needs, not theirs. They may want you to have a "successful career" in a well-known company, but this is your life, not theirs. We are constantly bombarded by powerful messages (from parents, bosses, authors!, celebrities, social media) about what we should be (smarter, stronger, richer) and about how to lead (empower, be authentic, walk the walk). Try not to be driven by fear or anxiety. A decision made from fear is rarely the right decision.

When you spend all your time running from one commitment to another, you never have time to just sit quietly and reflect. Give yourself time to reduce the noise and demands of the outer world and focus on what *you* want. You may well start from a place of uncertainty—exploit that uncertainty to drive your search for greater meaning.

However you get in touch with your purpose, let it shape your life. My father had a purpose to help young people fulfill their potential. He was a headmaster for twenty-one years, and it undoubtedly drove him, even if he didn't have a "purpose statement." My career followed an uncertain path until I discovered what I loved and ended up building a company as the vehicle for it. My wife, Jane, everyone's second mother, is helping young people navigate the difficult transition they face when trying to find their purpose and journey in life. She coaches young adults and is also a governor at a school for young people from troubled circumstances and special needs. Finding these purposes made all our lives more fulfilling. Make sure you find yours.

Reflections on Finding Your Purpose

1. Have you taken the time and space to really reflect on your purpose in life?

2. What impact are you trying to have?

3. What do you want your legacy to be?

CHAPTER 7

Being Authentic, Living Your Values

This above all; to thine own self be true.

—William Shakespeare, in *Hamlet*

I n chapter 5, we explored who you are and the importance of self-insight. Being *authentic* is about being that person with your team, partners, and clients. Or, to be more precise, being the best version of that person as much as humanly possible. We all have bad moments and bad days, right?

When I was a young manager, I tried very hard to be what I thought a manager *should* be. I tried to show conviction, for example. The trouble was, I sometimes did it when I didn't feel very sure of my ground. People almost certainly saw right through me. It wasn't until I attended a training program in my thirties when a wise American consultant wrote on a flip chart, "Bring who you are to what you do," that I finally felt free to be myself—and ask for help when I needed it. Or to simply say, "I don't know the right course of action—that's what we have to figure out." Totally liberating, and completely authentic.

On a deeper level, a helpful way of living and working in a way that feels aligned and healthy is to live your values. Values describe the qualities we feel are desirable, essential, useful, and worthwhile. They influence the direction of how we feel, think, and make choices, and how we perform and behave. Values have transformative energy. Your values shape—for better or worse—behaviors that can improve the lives of everyone around you. Values are what you feel and believe to be true, your accumulated wealth of experience.

Identifying and living in alignment with your personal values is helpful in many ways:

> *Finding your purpose*: Knowing your values helps you figure out what you want out of your life.

> *Guiding your behavior*: Values help you behave in a way that matches who you want to be.

> *Helping you make decisions*: When you're facing a decision, you can ask yourself what would be aligned with your values.

> *Increasing your confidence*: Identifying your values brings a sense of safety and stability into your life because you know what's important to you.

Do you know what you stand for? And do you put those values into practice on a daily basis? There are plenty of tools available online—lists of values, for example—for you to consider your response to this question. But in my experience, you really need to listen to your heart on this.

In her book, *Dare to Lead*, Brené Brown writes—

"Ask yourself:

> › Does this define me?
>
> › Is this who I am at my best?
>
> › Is this a filter that I use to make hard decisions?"[1]

My client and good friend Jan, with whom I have worked for many years, places a very high value on teamwork. It is one of the values that has united us in a common cause during the work we have done together over two decades. Every day at Tipico, Jan would walk around the office, each floor of the building, and greet people. He always knew their names, showed interest in them, and encouraged a sense of team. But he wasn't doing it artfully; he was just being himself.

By contrast, I was greeted with great courtesy by the CEO in the reception area of a very different business; his arrival in the morning coincided with my own. I followed him through a large, open-plan workspace, and we must have passed close to fifty people. He never looked at or greeted any of them, including his personal assistant. I spent that coaching session with my client exploring the impact of his behavior on those around him. He is actually a kind man who happens to be quite shy and whose values are around integrity, dependability, and fairness.

The first example shows how our values can positively power our leadership impact. The second shows that sometimes we have to step out of our comfort zone in order to avoid unintentionally creating the wrong kind of impact.

As a founder, I believe your personal values *should* inform your company values. What could be more powerful than an alignment between personal values, company values, and the values of your customers? This has a compounding effect. Elon Musk, talking about his SpaceX business, said, "You want to wake up in the morning and think the future is going to be great—and that's what being a spacefaring civilization is all about. It's about believing in the future and thinking that the future will be better than the past. And I can't think of anything more exciting than going out there and being among the stars."[2] The values of SpaceX are innovation, commitment, the visionary mindset, and conserving the planet. You don't need to know Elon personally to recognize that he strives to embody these values.

Living through our values is authentic leadership and gives power to our purpose. DuPont is world-renowned for its safety standards. As they say at DuPont, the key to safety is that "you get the level of safety performance and excellence that you, as a leader, personally demonstrate that you want."[3]

When it comes to values, leaders have to "go first," and in doing so, we can have a huge impact on everyone who comes after. We become the point of reference that everyone else adjusts to, and as a consequence, we are more likely to be followed than if we were to hang back. When leaders go first, they have a chance to set the example. There's no more powerful way to influence the behavior of our team than to physically demonstrate our readiness to behave that way, too.

The longer we lead, the more our team begins to reflect who we are, for better or worse. As the old adage says, "Children act like their parents—despite all attempts to teach them good manners."

Reflections on Being Authentic and Living Your Values

1. Do you know what your values are? Are you clear about what you stand for?

2. Have you audited how well you live these values on a daily basis?

3. Are your personal values reflected in the values of the business you founded?

4. Are you actively "going first" in order to influence others to make these values live on a daily basis?

CHAPTER 8

Embracing Humility

Mastery begins with humility.

—Robin Sharma, author

Jim Collins, in his renowned book *Good to Great*, said the "X" factor of great leadership is humility.[1] Superficially, it feels counterintuitive when so many of our role models as leaders are charismatic and bold. But humility matters because it enables us to see ourselves truthfully—to admit our doubts, face our fears, ask for help. In doing that, we build trust with those around us, which is essential for relationships and critical for leadership. The moment you ask for help is the moment your team will start working on the problem.

Some years ago, I was asked to go to Jordan to coach the CEO of one of that country's largest public companies. The CEO picked me up on his way to the office in his chauffeur-driven car. The driver called ahead to forewarn of his arrival, and the elevator was held for him to avoid a wait. A group of employees was waiting respectfully as we were ushered past them to his top-floor office with views over Amman. These were the perks of his position, ones that spoke to his power and importance within the company. I noticed that he saw very few people throughout the day. Only a select group of executives worked on the top floor, and he rarely interacted with other employees. I asked him, "How can you lead effectively if you don't know what people think?" It had never occurred to him. Leaders are always at risk of getting an inflated ego. And the bigger their ego grows, the more they are at risk of ending up in an insulated bubble, out of touch with their colleagues, their culture, and ultimately their clients, with potentially fatal consequences for their company. Think Dick Fuld (Lehman), Ken Lay (Enron), Fred Goodwin (RBS), and pretty much any company where the executives cut themselves off from the rest of the team and lived like royalty.

The tech startup culture is jam-packed with seemingly confident leaders, and all too easily, founder confidence morphs into founder arrogance. Staying humble means being aware of and admitting what you don't know. That shouldn't be hard on the face of it; what we don't know dwarfs what we know. It strongly suggests that we should focus on what we *do* know and go from there. Humility also means being OK with making mistakes and asking for help. When you are humble, you open yourself up to continuous growth and learning, and you prime yourself to handle the inevitable lows of startup life with some grace and dignity.

Being humble as a leader also makes you more relatable and approachable. It creates a work environment in which your team members will feel more comfortable being open, taking risks, and showing vulnerability themselves. The research backs this up. In a Chinese study involving nearly one thousand leaders and managers across sixty-three private companies, published in *Administrative Science Quarterly*, CEO humility was found to be "positively associated with empowering leadership behaviors, which in turn correlated with [top management team] integration."[2]

Another study, this time in the United States, looked at 105 privately held small to medium-sized firms in the computer software and hardware industry. The firms had under $5 million in revenue and less than five hundred employees.[3] They found that humble CEOs often create better financial returns for their companies. The researchers suggested that humble CEOs tend to encourage others to participate in decision-making and eliminate destructive self-interest and politics, all in favor of attaining a shared goal. In turn, this causes the top management team in the company to become more collaborative.

In his book *Humble Leadership*, Ed Schein says that as organizations face more complex interdependent tasks, leadership must become more personal in order to ensure open, trusting communication that will make more collaborative problem-solving and innovation possible.[4] For more *personal*, you can also read more *intimate*—see chapter 38 on trust.

In her 2017 TED Talk, Amy Edmondson describes the successful 2010 rescue attempt to save the lives of many Chilean miners who were trapped underground.[5] She noted three values that made the rescue team incredibly collaborative:

> The members of the rescue team were all humble—completing the mission was more important than being the person who had the idea.

> They were curious, asking questions about one another's experience and fully listening to the answers.

> They were free to take risks because their culture of collaboration meant that failure wasn't seen as losing to someone else but as trying to find a solution.

Humility contributed to saving the lives of all thirty-three trapped miners after sixty-nine days.

I've coached many founder leaders, and humility doesn't always come naturally to them. I suspect one of the problems is that to be a founder, you must have a vision of some kind to give people a sense of direction.

And that *requires* some ego. Unfortunately, that sometimes comes with a dose of false pride. Author and speaker Ken Blanchard has described how the ego gets in our way. People get too focused on self and self-worth—we think we are brighter or smarter than others. He calls this "Promoting Self." Conversely, we may have self-doubt and fear—he calls this "Protecting Self."[6] In both instances, we are comparing ourselves with others and distorting what is true. But as Rick Warren said, "Humility is not thinking less of yourself; it is thinking of yourself less."[7] Truly humble people think more of others. Humility tames our judgmental nature and motivates us to support and encourage others.

Humility is very advantageous for a leader in many ways. Adam Grant, in his book *Think Again*, writes: "The most effective leaders score high in both confidence AND humility. Although they have faith in their strengths, they're also keenly aware of their weaknesses. They know they need to recognize and transcend their limits if they want to push the limits of greatness."[8] Humility, he says, is a filter: It converts evidence and experience into knowledge and wisdom. A big ego does the opposite; it leads us to have a strong confirmation bias. As a result, we lose perspective and end up in a place where we only see and hear what we want to. We are "out of touch."

Without humility, leaders can be arrogant and set in their ways. They are prone to making avoidable mistakes, blaming others for their poor decisions, and overestimating their own talents to the point of losing touch with reality, preferring instead to surround themselves with "yes men." In leadership, few traits are as indicative of incompetence as arrogance. Unfortunately, as talent guru Tomas Chamorro-Premuzic points out, we are often seduced, if not blinded, by charisma. So, we gravitate toward entertaining showmen (yes, usually men) who are fearlessly charming in high-stakes settings and socially skilled to the point of violating conventional etiquette. "The problem is not that we find this enchanting, but that we equate it to leadership talent," he says.[9]

Reflections on Embracing Humility

1. Do you share what you don't know or are not sure about?

2. Do you ask for help when you need it?

3. Are you comfortable with making mistakes?

4. Do you support and encourage others to be similarly open, take risks, and show vulnerability?

5. Do you let others take the lead if they have the best ideas or experience?

6. Do you hire smart people with the confidence to speak up?

CHAPTER 9

Having the Courage to Be Different

Courage is the most important of all the virtues, because without courage you can't practice any other virtue consistently.

—Maya Angelou, speaking to the
2008 Cornell University graduating class

S imply to start a business requires courage. It is a risk. We tend to forget that a job is a risk, too, and in that case, all your eggs are in one
basket. In spite of this underlying truth, starting a business is likely
to have real and immediate financial and other consequences for you in a
way that a job does not. Most people are unwilling to quit their stable jobs
to pursue a risky venture. You can't blame them—nine out of ten startups
fail, and we all have bills to pay.

Steve Wozniak, Henry Ford, and Sarah Blakely built Apple, Ford, and
Spanx—all while working a nine-to-five job to begin with. I found my

own way to reduce the risk of leaving my salary behind. I negotiated a consultancy contract that would give me a baseline income for the early period of my new life. Despite this, I was still fearful. My daughter had just been born, and we moved into a bigger house at exactly the same time we launched Value Partnership. However, here I am some twenty-five years later, sharing our story and richer in every sense for the experience. I was afraid to fail, and that made me all the more determined to succeed.

Entrepreneurs face plenty of risks and uncertainties, and not just at the beginning of the journey. The decision to hire expensive talent. The decision to raise capital. The decision to IPO. Courage is a critical psychological resource for entrepreneurs. Without courage, an individual may never follow through with an entrepreneurial idea or leave the perks and certainties of traditional employment to pursue entrepreneurship in the first place. Courage means having the strength to step outside of your comfort zone and risk failure. In fact, if you are going to be brave, then you will *know* failure—it's inevitable.

The good news is that courage is not binary; it's not either present or absent. And it can be built over time. The first time you run a marathon or jump out of a plane, it's scary. But every time you repeat it, familiarity and experience make it easier. The founder's journey requires you to find your courage in every moment and deepen your well of courage over time. Since you cannot control the outcome, all you can do is keep showing up, keep taking forward steps.

Try to seize the moment whenever you can. Procrastination is a way of putting off the risk of failure. How nice to tell people about your bold plans—how much harder to tell them that you have started and it isn't going as well as you had hoped. You don't have a boss who is setting deadlines for you, so you may have to create your own. Try not to fear failure; the truth is that the only real failure is not seizing your moment at all.

Whitney Wolfe Herd, the founder of Bumble, designed the dating app so only women can send the first message when users match on the platform.

In an online dating environment where women experience routine harassment, she aspired to create a safer space for digital romance. In a 2021 *Time* magazine article, she says, "I've never had this healthy male relationship until I created it. I engineered an ecosystem of healthy male relationships in my life."[1]

Wolfe Herd is a very purpose-driven founder. Speaking at her IPO, she promised to "try and make the Internet a kinder, more accountable place." Her better-known male counterparts don't tend to think like this. More than relationships, friendships, or in-app purchases, Wolfe Herd sees Bumble as giving "the feeling of power to the powerless, a sense of order in an online universe that so frequently seems lawless."[2]

Founders like this back themselves when others around them do not get it. They don't wait for a trend to follow it; they anticipate it or see it before others do. And then they act on that conviction. This, too, is courage.

Sometimes even deeper levels of courage are required. One of my clients had built an early-stage team with close personal friends in some key roles. My engagement came at the moment he had begun to realize that this was no longer working and, in fact, was holding the business back. Facing into the truth of this and having those honest conversations with his friends was in everybody's best interests. But it required guts. Those friendships are still intact today, by the way.

As I write, I am supporting a founder CEO who had built a team of ninety doing some amazing work in the tech world. Unfortunately, the timing of their need for more capital coincided with a collapse in the fundraising environment. It couldn't have come at a worse time. On Monday, he has to tell two-thirds of them that their jobs are "at risk." The need for courage is everywhere for founders. Of course, you'll seek to avoid these situations. But don't kid yourself; there will be hard moments, and you need to be prepared for that. As Nelson Mandela once said, "I learned that courage was not the absence of fear, but the triumph over it."[3]

Reflections on Having the Courage to Be Different

1. Do you have a readiness to take risks, step outside your comfort zone, and fail?

2. Do you have a tendency to procrastinate and the capacity to overcome it?

3. Do you have the capacity to act with conviction in the face of uncertainty, to lead rather than follow a trend?

4. How ready are you to face into the inevitable difficulties you have already faced or will face in the future?

5. How ready are you to allow members of your team to take risks, step outside their comfort zone, and fail?

CHAPTER 10

Developing Resilience and Discipline

Build resilience in yourselves. When tragedy or disappointment strike, know that you have the ability to get through absolutely anything. I promise you do.

—Sheryl Sandberg, *Lean In*

S tarting and growing a business will get tough. Disappointments will sap your confidence. And in the early stages, you will feel a bit of a fraud at times. In 1998, as we got our leadership consultancy off the ground, we used a small virtual office in London where we could book a room for a client meeting if we needed one. On short notice, we were asked to meet the CEO of a FTSE100 company at our offices in London. We booked the best room with about thirty minutes on either side of the scheduled time for safety, in case we had to start early or run late. On the day of the meeting, the CEO's driver called to say he was running more than an hour early. I was in a meeting in another location and had to hustle to get to our offices. Desperation ensued as we tried to acquire the room earlier and persuade another group to vacate it. It was a very stressful day, but we impressed the CEO enough to secure the work. Hustling is what you need to be ready for in the early days.

As the business starts to become established, things will change—but they won't necessarily get any easier. Resilience will still be required. In other words, that quality that allows someone to be knocked down by the adversities of life and come back at least as strong as before. Easier said than done, but help is at hand. Dr. Julie Smith, in her book *Why Has Nobody Told Me This Before?*, gives us seven tips to beat what she calls "low mood":

> Exercise, especially if it is regular

> Social connection, rather than private rumination

> Intention setting, clarify what you need to do

> Pleasurable activity, whatever you enjoy

> Gratitude practice, focus on what you appreciate each day

> Sleep, achieving your best sleep pattern

> Nutrition, healthy eating habits[1]

In many ways, this links back to what we explored in chapter 3: time, energy, and focus. Understanding how we think/feel is *not* evidence that our thoughts/feelings are true. Just because you feel deflated about how a pitch went doesn't mean it went badly. And it certainly doesn't mean that you are bad at pitching. When negative thoughts appear, we need to gain some distance from them to evaluate what is and isn't true. I help clients gain this distance and perspective in coaching very frequently, as we are all inclined to fall into this trap. Those thoughts typically don't stand up to scrutiny. What is the story you are telling yourself? And does it enable you to keep learning and growing?

We have direct control over our level of resilience in the sense that what we think and feel is directly impacted by the choices we make every day. If you work long hours, eat fast food, don't make time for exercise, and get little sleep, don't be surprised if you experience low moods that are hard to break out from. This significantly reduces your resilience.

Less within our control is the VUCA world we live in (VUCA: volatile, uncertain, complex, ambiguous). Dr. Lynda Folan, in a recent *People Management* article, argues that leaders need strong self-awareness, an internal locus of control, and constructive thinking. Dr. Folan goes on to point out that leaders also need to develop *organizational resilience* to survive adversity and thrive in a world of uncertainty.[2] More on this in a later chapter.

Author Roselinde Torres has written and spoken about what makes a great twenty-first-century leader. She argues that it's a vital question because it isn't credible to think that the twenty-first-century demands we face can be tackled with twentieth-century leadership. "So, what makes a great leader in the twenty-first century? I've met many, and they stand out. They are women and men who are preparing themselves not for the comfortable predictability of yesterday but also for the realities of today and all of those unknown possibilities of tomorrow," says Torres.[3]

Torres argues that we need the ability to see around corners to avoid being surprised by the next market shift. That ability is enhanced by exploring topics that will inform that understanding, building diverse professional networks, and being courageous enough to abandon the past. Can you let go of familiar practices that have kept you afloat in the past, but no longer serve you or your company? How open are you to hearing criticism from close peers about your ideas?

Where does discipline fit in? It helps you to be resilient. Stay focused on your end goal and recognize that it is hard work over a sustained period that will bring success, not easy or quick fixes. Small steps eventually lead to the top of the mountain. And if the top of the mountain seems a long way off,

FOUNDER'S LEGACY

break the journey into bite-sized chunks and celebrate milestones. I always find it easier to count down the last few miles of a marathon. "Only three miles to go" feels a lot better than "This is the twenty-fourth mile"!

Value the small things, not just the big ones. One travel industry leader I know insists on regularly doing the operational things that matter alongside team members, like standing at the airport holding the sign that welcomes guests. Show your team that you value every contribution, however small it seems.

Just as when you were a child, your parents may have made you make your bed every morning to teach you self-discipline, make sure you bring good housekeeping into your working life as a founder. It's partly to manage your energy well, and partly because every team member is watching your example. Keep your promises to yourself and to your team. Show them that self-discipline and integrity matter.

Reflections on Resilience and Discipline

1. How can you make smart daily choices to take care of your energy levels, in areas like sleep, exercise, and nutrition?

2. How can you make sure, with the help of others, that the story you tell yourself powers your growth?

3. Do you recognize the need to build organizational resilience into your team and organization?

4. How might you explore topics that will enable you to anticipate the future, build diverse professional networks, and abandon the past?

5. How can you bring discipline to the steps that you need to take every day to achieve longer-term success?

6. In what ways can you role model the self-discipline you would like to encourage in others?

Avoiding the "Founder's Trap"

*There are only two lasting bequests we can hope to give our children.
One of these is roots, the other, wings.*

—Johann Wolfgang von Goethe

P arents, in the end, have to let their children go. Once we have given
them "roots and wings," we need to let them fly. Sometimes the same
applies to the companies we found.

There is no doubt that if the business survives the perilous early
stages of its life, the founder's mentality will have played an important
role. Chris Zook and James Allen, in their book *The Founder's Mentality,*
describe how founder-led companies that grow profitably to scale often
consider themselves insurgents, waging war on their industry on behalf
of underserved customers.[1] Such founder-led companies possess a clear
sense of mission. They foster deep feelings of personal responsibility for
the company among their employees. They abhor complexity and bureaucracy. They are obsessed with the details of the business and celebrate the

frontline employees who deal directly with customers. My sense is that this is broadly true—all the founders I coach have this sense of mission and commitment to their cause.

However, the behaviors and practices that work in the early stages of a business rarely translate once the company reaches a certain point of maturity. That's why you hear of so many founders being replaced as CEO once institutional investors join the board. The term *founder's trap*, first coined by Dr. Ichak Adizes in his book *Corporate Lifecycles*, describes the moment when, despite their best intentions, founders begin to inhibit growth and success through their inexperience, lack of knowledge, mindset, or pattern of behavior.[2] At this point, founders should choose to either keep control but face the need for change or hand the business over to someone better equipped to take the business to the next level.

So, what causes the "trap," when does it typically happen, and how can we avoid falling into it?

Once over the "hurdles" of the initial startup period of a new business, founders find themselves in the growth phase. This requires a shift from the founders and core team doing everything to bringing in some hired professional help. Funding shifts from early stage to growth capital.

Leadership needs to come to the fore as, while the business model may well be proven, the ability to scale is now the challenge. Sometimes the founder struggles to delegate effectively or hire the talent required to take the business to the next level, or finds the new level of strategic management required hard to master. At worst, the pace of growth and progress—and the results they had dreamed of—begin to evaporate.

But is this actually a trap—or an opportunity for learning and growth? Andrew Hill's 2019 article in the *Financial Times* described "the torment of founders who cannot let go of their babies" and the entrepreneurial founders' desire to succeed as an "elemental force."[3] Without this mindset, where's the drive, passion, and energy required to take the organization to the next level? However, it's precisely these emotions that can create problems. And during a growth period, more reflective founders start to realize their own limitations. Once the founder no longer feels in control of the business, investors may start to push for the appointment of a new CEO.

Noam Wasserman wrote what became a famous paper for the Academy of Management in 2006 called "Rich versus King: The Entrepreneur's Dilemma." The paper looks at how a person's motivation for financial gain can directly conflict with his or her desire for control. As the author says, "The entrepreneur will have to choose between attracting the resources that will help build a valuable company, in the process giving up a lot of equity and decision-making control, or else retain equity and control while not being able to build as valuable a company."[4] Rarely can entrepreneurs attain both. Wasserman looked at 457 American technology startups from the 2000s. His analysis showed that founders maximized the value of their equity stakes by *giving up* the CEO position and board control: "The results show that the more decision-making control kept (at both the CEO and board levels), the lower the value of the entrepreneur's equity stake. Thus, entrepreneurs are more likely to grow a more valuable venture if they are willing to give up control, or they can keep control, not attract the best resources (people, capital) to the venture, and be more likely to end up with less-valuable stakes."[5]

The choice, however, is not as binary as the *founder's trap* term suggests. It *is* possible for a founder to continue to lead their business successfully into the future. I know founders of fast-growth, agile organizations at this stage in the development of their business who were able to adapt to the demands of being CEO, some who didn't, and some who didn't want to and instead stepped aside or shifted into a different leadership role. What is the right option? Every circumstance has its own characteristics. My experience suggests that leadership coaching can unlock problems and expose opportunities for the founder, in some cases transitioning them successfully into the CEO role. The business is in safe hands and retains the founder's passion and vision—a potentially win-win situation.

Rob Small, then CEO of Miniclip, was feeling "trapped" back in 2013 when the business flatlined. He and I worked together to strengthen his leadership team in key positions and worked on how to forge a common purpose, goals, and road map to unlock growth. The business grew rapidly under his continuing stewardship and was ultimately acquired, thus realizing his aspirations for the business. He grew enormously as a person and became an excellent CEO. Less "trap," more "opportunity" in his case.

The best way to approach the decision of how to navigate the founder's trap is to seek counsel from those around you and ask the fundamental question: What is in the best interests of the business? What will help us to make greater progress toward our vision and purpose? If the answer involves someone else leading the business, then perhaps it's time to stand aside. Jack Dorsey, founder and former CEO of Twitter, put it this way: "There's a lot of talk about the importance of a company being 'founder led.' Ultimately, I believe that's severely limiting and a single point of failure. . . . I believe it's critical a company can stand on its own, free of its founder's influence or direction."[6]

LinkedIn co-founder Reid Hoffman hired and successfully partnered with CEO Jeff Weiner at LinkedIn five years after the company's foundation. In a 2013 LinkedIn post, Hoffman suggests that founders ask themselves, "What am I focused on? What am I world-class at? What am I really committed to?" He goes on to say, "In my experience, CEOs need to derive satisfaction from the nuts and bolts of building a company, not just building product and articulating the vision. They need to be passionate about leadership, management, and organizational processes as the company scales."[7] While Hoffman is right, for many founders, it simply isn't the case. Since you are reading this book, I imagine that you *do* have an interest in these areas.

In choosing the path forward, Hoffman also considered the alternative to hiring a CEO: remaining in charge as founder CEO and hiring a chief operating officer (COO) to run the operating business and ensure execution of the strategy. This might work if the partnership is founded on a strong basis of trust and mutual respect. It will not work if it's simply off-loading things that you as founder CEO are disinterested in.

An exceptional founder CEO might be able to lead the company to success, and that's a very appealing prospect in principle. In my experience, if that person has a growth mindset and sufficient interest in every aspect of the business, like Rob at Miniclip, then at minimum, it extends the duration of this leadership.

The Founder's Mentality research highlights that success is not simply down to a person; it's about a mindset—a mindset that non-founder CEOs would do well to adopt.

Reflections on Avoiding the "Founder's Trap"

1. Do you have conviction about how to lead the business through the next stage of its evolution?

2. Are you prepared to consider stepping aside or focusing your role on where you add the most value?

3. What decision is in the long-term interests of the business? What will best enable it to fulfill its enduring purpose?

CHAPTER 12

Acting as Steward

Character is crucial: A Berkshire CEO must be "all in" for the company, not for himself.

—Warren Buffett[1]

A s you build a team of directors, you will start to have expectations of them. You will want them and their teams to perform well individually, but you will also want them to put the interests of the company ahead of their unit or function. What you want is stewardship.

For example, the CEO of a circular fashion business I worked with felt her growing team was too focused on their functional agendas. If they were going to take the business to the next level, the team needed to be strongly aligned around purpose, vision, and values, and they needed to learn how to operate with both individual and mutual accountability. The CEO and team needed to do the following:

> Provide collective leadership to the business as a whole—thinking like CEOs.

> Build a strategy that delivers on the company's purpose and vision for all its stakeholders.

> Live the company's values, role modelling its DNA, championing diversity and inclusion.

> Maximize the accountability, collaboration, and impact of one another and other leaders across the business.

> Enable people to work together to accelerate the company's growth.

The CEO expected this pattern of behavior from her colleagues on a consistent basis, supported by intermittent team coaching. By raising collective awareness of "the problem," agreeing what the "better" pattern of behavior would look like, and regular practice and feedback, the team raised its game. They increased performance in all of the aforementioned areas over a year—and by as much as 30 percent on "thinking like CEOs." It took a lot of pressure off the CEO and improved cross-functional collaboration significantly.

There is tremendous power in an aligned team taking responsibility for the overall health and performance of the business. It really doesn't make sense that all that responsibility is left to one person in the CEO chair. Leaders who put the interests of their firm above their own is a tenet of the "stewardship theory" first introduced by Lex Donaldson and James Davis in 1989. According to stewardship theory, owners don't *really* own a company; they only hold it in trust. And if that company has a higher purpose, then it is the achievement of that purpose that should determine the right course of action, not simply the authority or shares of the founder CEO.[2]

A sense of stewardship teaches you that your business isn't about you. This mindset implies that you are holding the business in trust for some higher principle; purpose-driven founders naturally embrace this approach because the purpose is more important than personal interests. For example, in September 2022, Yvon Chouinard, founder of Patagonia, announced that he was relinquishing ownership of the company he founded nearly fifty years before.[3] Patagonia is now owned by two legal entities that will ensure that

(1) the company continues to operate on the purpose and values Chouinard embedded from the beginning, and (2) any money that isn't reinvested into Patagonia will be used to support people and organizations that are dedicated to protecting the planet (an estimated $100 million annually).

Even if your principal interest is profit, however, it still makes sense to put the interests of the company (its profitability) ahead of your own personal interests. Stewardship theory also drives you to keep the company in good shape for when the next leader or owner takes over.

There is a story (probably apocryphal) about an upstream process manager at a major European oil firm who found a way to improve the performance of their unit in the short term. The manager's career took a major leap forward as a result, and they moved him up and away from the unit. The replacement leader, however, found it impossible to sustain the improved level of performance, and process performance problems increasingly impacted downstream areas. The former manager was quickly summoned back and instructed to "fix it." His promotion was canceled. Lesson learned, hopefully—never put your own short-term interests first in this company!

Being a formal company director brings with it stewardship responsibilities. Legally speaking, company directors have a duty to put the interests of the company first; this isn't discretionary, and not doing it will land you in the justice system. The UK's Companies Act 2006 specifies that company directors must "act in the way you consider, in good faith, would be most likely to promote the success of the company for the benefit of its members as a whole." The act defines success as having regard for the following:

> "The likely consequences of any decision in the long term

> The interests of the company's employees

> The need to foster the company's business relationships with suppliers, customers, and others

> The impact of the company's operations on the community and the environment

> The desirability of the company maintaining a reputation for high standards of business conduct

> The need to act fairly as between members of the company"[4]

Remember, this is simply the legal framework—you can set the bar higher to embrace your purpose, values, and business ambition. Expect that from your team.

I say this to elevate your sense of agency as founder, shareholder, and CEO, and to encourage you to keep your purpose in mind and your ego in check; every other stakeholder will look to you for leadership as you tackle the myriad of challenges you face trying to grow your business. As the business becomes a wider community, your role, contribution, and significance will change fundamentally. In fact, for a startup to successfully grow, it *must* become an institution that transcends any one individual. To leave a legacy that will serve those that follow, founders need to know it's OK to let go and build others to take over.

Reflections on Acting as Steward

1. How are you doing on putting the company's needs first?

2. Are you actively seeking to create a company-first mindset in your team?

3. Are you putting the company and its purpose ahead of personal needs where necessary to enable your business to thrive and evolve?

4. Are you considering your succession and/or trying to reduce the dependence of the business on you in the interests of its longer-term health?

PART II

THE JOB OF
A LEADER

CHAPTER 13

Being the Founder CEO

Look—this is the terror of being a founder and CEO. It is all your fault. Every decision, every person you hire, every dumb thing you buy or do—ultimately, you're at the end.

—Ben Horowitz, co-founder and general partner
at the venture capital firm Andreessen Horowitz

Ben goes on to say, "The thing that's confusing for investors is that founders don't know how to be CEO. I didn't know how to do the job when I was a CEO. Founder CEOs don't know how to be CEOs, but it doesn't mean they can't learn. The question is . . . can the founder learn that job and can they tolerate all the mistakes they will make doing it?"[1]

So, what is the role of the CEO? I think there is a straightforward answer to this question, which is useful, but also a specific answer that is even more useful, and each founder needs to figure the latter for themselves, depending on the nature of their business and where it is in its growth journey. Let me explain what I mean.

We are coming out of an era of "move fast and break things" where the combination of breakthrough technologies and free-flowing capital has made many CEOs household names. These include Adam Neumann at WeWork, Sam Bankman-Fried at FTX, and Charlie Javice, the young founder and former CEO of Frank. Javice sold her fintech startup to JP Morgan Chase for $175 million by creating a list of more than four million college-aged users that didn't exist. These CEOs all came with big promises and even bigger egos. And their stories perfectly illustrate the damage that unchecked power can do. They governed without the usual checks and balances, either because of their shareholding or through their personal magnetism. Their presumed genius led to unchecked loyalty from multiple stakeholders. People won't risk speaking truth to power—an age-old story. When failure comes, it's already too late, and when things unravel, they unravel at breakneck speed.

So, as I have explored in the first section of the book, the founder CEO should beware of a lack of humility or an inability to really listen to the people around them. The business is best served by a high-performing team rather than a cult.

So, to the straightforward answer, what is the role of the founder CEO? Let's look at seven things that are likely to be pivotal:

> Ensure the business has a clear and inspiring purpose, culture, and vision, and a strategy that your team is committed to delivering on that will realize those fundamentals over time. This strategic leadership role is at the heart of a purpose-driven founder's role.

> Set the standard for product/operational excellence. Make sure the business model is smart. Whatever the product or service offering, satisfy yourself that it is meeting a real market/customer need and that the execution is being done at a competitive price/quality level that provides for commercial success. Frequent customer interaction will be an essential part of this.

> Manage revenue, expenses, and external financing. Do not allow the business to run out of cash. It's the golden rule: You only run out of

cash once. Don't be deceived by growth or profitability; a growing business consumes cash for things like people and inventory. You need to lead the fundraising effort. If you have a CFO, great, but make sure you, as CEO, understand the cash implications of the business decisions that you make.

> Secure the right people in the right roles who perform well and create a powerful sense of team. This is hugely important, and you neglect it at your peril. Over time, getting the team right becomes getting the organization right and ensuring the culture is distinctive and a source of competitive advantage. Smart investors will not invest unless you have the right team in place.

> Attend to stakeholder management and governance. The moment your startup requires outside capital, you need to choose the right partners and manage the relationship with your shareholders. If you establish a board, you will have that relationship to manage, too, particularly the relationship with the chairman. There may be critical partnerships that also expect your attention—ones that drive business growth. You will need to help negotiate them. And your purpose and/or sector will determine which other organizations require attention, such as a regulator or certain NGOs.

> Promote your company's brand, products, and reputation. You are the primary spokesperson and ambassador for the business, and you will want to present a strong, positive story to relevant stakeholders. Building and maintaining a strong brand is a product of thought leadership and relationship management. Much of the future value of your company will be embedded in the brand that you must play a crucial role in building.

> Ensure your business adapts as it grows and the environment changes. All of the aforementioned requires constant attention to how the business context is changing and what that means for the

work of the organization. In chapter 25, we explore the role of the CEO in ensuring the team and the business change and innovate in pursuit of their purpose.

Beyond these fundamentals, the CEO role will depend a lot on the specifics of your business. My role in Value Partnership included particular emphasis on four areas:

> Business development

> Knowledge, culture, and organization

> People and talent management

> Brand building

Our business is hugely dependent on the quality and alignment of our team in delivering on our brand promise. The people are the product.

Another business, another type of CEO. Technology startups typically require a strong focus on the product, technology platform, partnerships, and player/user experience. Fashion businesses are about design, branding, manufacturing/supply chain, and community building. Depending on the nature of the business and your particular strengths as CEO, the role will need to be tailored for the best fit.

Remember that the demands of the job will change over time—in chapter 16, we explore the journey of the business from startup to reinvention. At each stage, the demands on the CEO evolve, and the adaptability of the CEO is an integral part of the evolution of the business. So, for example, in the early stages, the founder CEO will be involved in a lot of practical areas such as client relationship management and product development. Further on in the journey, with a team of specialists in place, the management requirements of the role are significant, and strategy demands more attention. Make sure you are aligned with your board on the contributions and performance impact you should have as CEO.

Reflections on Being the Founder CEO

1. What are the core demands of the role for *your* business? Do you have a written role description?

2. How will you make sure that each of these demands get the right amount of focused attention?

3. What are you strong at—where do you really add value as the founder CEO? What is like "play" to you?

4. What are you less interested in and pay less attention to? How are you going to ensure that those areas still get the quality attention they deserve?

CHAPTER 14

Embracing Dimensions of Leadership

Innovative leadership is essentially anchored on the leader's overall multifaceted resourcefulness and multidimensional competencies.

—Pearl Zhu, author[1]

So, in the middle of this book about leadership, there is a chapter about leadership. Why?

Here I describe four dimensions of leadership. In my experience, people tend to associate leadership with only one or two of these—and I would like to kill off that idea. Leadership is a multidimensional challenge, and leaders need to embrace all of them at different times. Let's explore each of them briefly.

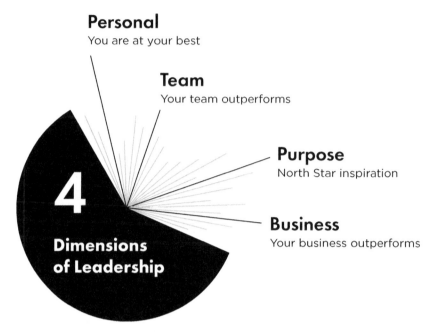

Figure 14.1. Image by permission of Value Partnership Ventures Ltd
and Value Partnership Ltd. All rights reserved.

PERSONAL LEADERSHIP

Understanding who you are as a leader and how to show up in the best
shape possible is the foundation for leadership. I have talked about leadership fundamentals quite a bit in the first section of the book. Successful
leaders know where their *natural inclinations* lie and use this knowledge to
boost those inclinations or compensate for them.

Being emotionally connected within yourself is hugely empowering.
It leads to conviction and better choices. An experienced leader but new
CEO who was excessively detail-oriented said to me at the end of our
coaching relationship, "I now feel that I am leading the business. I have
stepped up and am less worried about the detail. I now provide my team
with a strong business narrative and ensure a good platform is in place to
deliver that narrative. I am now clear, concise, and unapologetic."

In short, personal leadership involves the following commitments:

> Know yourself.

> Be true to your purpose.

> Lead through your values.

> Make smart time and stakeholder choices.

> Allow for recovery and learning.

TEAM LEADERSHIP

This is the art of building a high-performing team. A team needs to be fit for purpose. That purpose evolves as the business grows and the environment changes. A startup faces different challenges than a mature business. A crisis requires a different kind of response—often hard for a team that is used to good times and growth.

Founders cannot do it all themselves; they are not scalable. Beware of trying to become an octopus! Founders need to build a team that shares their purpose and values and can work together to build and execute a strategy for growth. Smart leaders tend to surround themselves with very talented people. Just as an orchestra conductor is tasked with optimizing and harmonizing the efforts of each musician to create something greater than discrete individual performances, leaders need to do the same.

When you look at high-performing teams in action (e.g., a Formula 1 team), you can see the evidence of hard work and practice. Why do we think business teams just click? We need to work at it, and that's the subject of chapter 38.

In short, team leadership involves the following steps:

> Assembling a talented and diverse team

> Establishing team disciplines and trust

> Giving space and expecting results

> Caring about your people

> Motivating through play, purpose, and potential (see chapter 31)

PURPOSE LEADERSHIP

Here we focus on the role of a leader in providing a purpose and creating a culture that gives meaning and a beating heart to the organization. Purpose is the "North Star" by which to steer your organization. It must inform your every decision, from the smallest to the life-changing. When things get rocky, it's a beacon to guide you out of trouble and get you back on track. (More on this in the next chapter.)

Purpose attracts customers and helps to deliver financial performance. Employees work harder, smarter, longer, more generously, and more productively when they can see how their work affects others. It's up to leaders to figure out how to connect people's work to the higher purpose. We know that purpose can get lost in the day-to-day pressures of running a business. Leaders, therefore, need to show up consistently to demonstrate their unwavering commitment.

Building a unifying culture that is distinctive and serves your business is also a powerful source of value creation. This is the subject of chapters 19 and 20.

In short, purpose leadership involves the following actions:

> Creating North Star inspiration

> Building a unifying culture

> Driving conviction-led change

> Showing grit in the face of uncertainty

> Fostering constant learning

EMBRACING DIMENSIONS OF LEADERSHIP

BUSINESS LEADERSHIP

This is the role of a leader in providing the strategy and road map the organization needs to achieve its purpose. Defining your business strategy is always tricky because the competitive environment is complex, uncertain, and dynamic, and your strategy needs to be as simple as possible. Experience teaches us that it's all about choosing the area you want to compete in, understanding it deeply, and then shaping your strategy to meet your business vision and goals. Sometimes, it's a case of choosing what *not* to do, while at other times it means a complete reimagining of the way forward.

Business leadership is not just about good strategy (chapter 21). It's also about execution, as we will explore in chapter 22, and creating the space for your team to perform. Do you have the business model, organization, and talent to succeed? You have to build them, just as you have to train for a marathon or any other challenge of substance.

A game development business I'm working with is currently struggling to deliver a game that is their first of its genre, their first using live testing, and their first GAAS (games as a service) game. In fact, it involves six "firsts," and they are now realizing that they may have bitten off more than they can chew. They describe it as a Jenga tower that is too tall—so they want to glue down some layers before adding more blocks. There are far too many concurrent issues to be solved.

In short, business leadership involves the following skills:

> Ensuring clear, strategic focus

> Building the capability to deliver

> Establishing performance accountability

> Fostering agility

> Sustaining a strong bias for action

Leadership is a multidimensional challenge, and I have described four clusters of behaviors and actions that can add value.

Reflections on Embracing the Dimensions of Leadership

1. Which of these four leadership dimensions do you recognize as a part of your practice?

2. Which represent strengths of yours?

3. Where do you need to raise your game?

CHAPTER 15

Orientating the Business

*Life is about perspective and how you look at something . . .
ultimately, you have to zoom out.*

—Whitney Wolfe Herd, founder of Bumble[1]

There are times as a leader when you need to be close to things, to your product, to the technology, to your customers and employees—in the "engine room" where details matter. This is being zoomed in. There are also times when you need to gain perspective, think big, and look to the future. This is being zoomed out, and that is what I would like you to do now.

One of the hardest things about leadership, especially for first-time CEOs, is figuring out the right path to take to grow your business. You face a myriad of choices, constraints, and pressures. At times, those pressures feel overwhelming. One leader I worked with described his experience like being a triage nurse trying to figure out what needed immediate attention and what could wait. But leadership is about much more than responding to pressures, of course. Leadership is fundamentally about going on a journey to a purposeful destination. This chapter, as well as the next one, is about that journey. What if you could clearly position your business on the journey and understand what to expect from the next stage? It would enable you to see into the future and be prepared for it. It might also highlight what needs attention right now.

In 2018, the Value Partnership team and I carried out research into the leadership challenges companies face when trying to grow and scale. What emerged was a nonlinear framework charting the main characteristics of the growth journey (figures 15.1 and 15.2). Take a moment to examine the figures and consider where your business sits today.

The Business Growth Journey

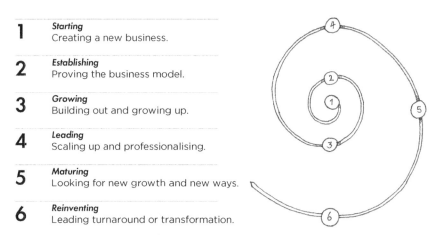

1   *Starting*
Creating a new business.

2   *Establishing*
Proving the business model.

3   *Growing*
Building out and growing up.

4   *Leading*
Scaling up and professionalising.

5   *Maturing*
Looking for new growth and new ways.

6   *Reinventing*
Leading turnaround or transformation.

Figure 15.1. Image by permission of Value Partnership Ventures Ltd and Value Partnership Ltd. All rights reserved.

STAGES IN THE BUSINESS GROWTH JOURNEY

1. Starting

Creating a new business: The idea takes shape. It is funded by self and/or family/friends. It is that moment when the idea or opportunity first presents itself. It's driven by passion and a belief in what is possible. It is the classic entrepreneur stage of high risk and potential high reward.

2. Establishing

Proving the business model: This is the proof of concept stage. It's the first 24 months. 80% of new start-ups fold within this timescale so it's all about proving the basics of the model work. It will lead to first round funding as part of it. It's really about the idea finding its direction and getting into revenue and carefully managing cash. The founders and a few new employees are doing everything.

3. Growing

Building out and growing up: Out of proof-of-concept and moving into being an established business. Pushing hard to grow market share and scale. This is the key stage that requires the shift from the founders and core team doing everything to bringing in some hired help. Funding shifts from early stage to growth capital. Leadership needs to come to the fore, as whilst the business model may well be proven, the ability to scale is the challenge.

4. Leading

Scaling up and professionalizing: Ownership of the category for the business emerges. From a 'surviving to thriving' mindset where growth issues are the main challenge. How to scale and build the business and its professionalization whilst preserving its original mindset and the culture that made it successful in the first place. From a funding point of view this could be classic mainstream private equity territory or a strategic investor decides to buy and invest (to help capitalize on the position the business has established). Leadership shifts towards a much more strategic agenda, with M&A also an option.

continued

5. Maturing

Looking for new growth and new ways: No longer the 'new kid on the block', 5–7 years into the game and critical mass has been established. Looking for the next wave of growth starts to pre-occupy the leadership. Maintaining market leadership becomes harder as there is share to lose. The culture of the organization feels grown up and far removed from the earlier stages. It probably needs a different type of leadership altogether. The trick is to find new growth or re-invent. Steady state leads to loss of momentum or decline. Capital is required to find new sources of growth. Finding the right talent to challenge the current business or culture is a balancing act to get right.

6. Reinventing

Leading turnaround or transformation: The business/corporation has hit a plateau and not managed to move out of maturing. It's turnaround or transformation territory and in all likelihood new leadership is required. It's been marked by a failure to keep the business moving forward. The business is almost certainly owned by private equity or is listed and the tension with managing the shareholder dynamic is often adversarial. This is where the business needs to change significantly its market, product, leadership and culture.

Figure 15.2. Image by permission of Value Partnership Ventures Ltd and Value Partnership Ltd. All rights reserved.

It's OK to be a bit unsure; this framework has its limits. At best, it describes the journey in broad brushstrokes. And the timescales mentioned may be wrong because of the characteristics of your particular sector. Some businesses in high-growth sectors take off like a rocket and accelerate quickly through the stages, while others take a more measured pace.

It's also true to say that some businesses get stuck. For example, stage 3: Growing, when the business seeks to scale, is often a particularly challenging phase to successfully navigate. Some businesses are much more scalable than others. For example, software companies are typically highly scalable and talent-dependent businesses less so. The truth is that founders sometimes fall into the trap of believing that the things that got us this far will continue to bring success through the growth stage. And they don't. There are ladders that need to be built to move to the next level, snakes that need to be avoided lest you fall back.

One founder CEO, who was a natural game changer, couldn't help but continually innovate around products and markets. But his investors were looking for faster growth. His costly (in time and money) diversification attempts were a distraction from the much more focused growth strategy required for the core business to strengthen its grip on the market and improve its financial position. The CEO was still operating in stage 2; the business needed stage 3 leadership. Since I was his coach, it was my job to help him see that and help him to find a new approach that unlocked faster growth but still exploited his innovative contribution.

As Ben Horowitz (of VC firm Andreessen Horowitz) explains in his book *The Hard Thing About Hard Things*, effective CEOs must both know what to do and be able to get their companies to do those things. He argues that founding CEOs are generally much better at the first part than the second and, as a result, they often struggle as their organizations grow and become more complex.[2] While many people talk about how great it is to start a business, very few are honest about how difficult it is to run one.

In the early stages, the CEO is working on pitching the idea, developing the product and technology, assembling a team, winning customers, and creating a brand. Over time, the challenges evolve into working on strategy, streamlining operations, and managing an increasing number of employees, products, services, functions, geographies, and customers. These challenges have little in common with the leadership requirements of a startup. Post-IPO, the increased visibility and dispersed ownership only further complicate the CEO role.

So, as founder CEOs, we need to be very aware of where we are in the unfolding story of our enterprise—and ready to adjust to meet the changing demands as they arise. Zooming out can help us do that.

That leads us to the next question: What are the main leadership imperatives for the business journey, and how do they change along the pathway described in this chapter? Now that we have orientated our business, we need a compass to guide our business along that pathway. That is the subject of the next chapter.

Reflections on Orientating the Business

1. At what stage in the business journey do you think you are? (1–6)

2. What are the implications of that insight for how you lead the business?

3. Are you ready to consider the adjustments that you may need to make in how you lead?

CHAPTER 16

Navigating Your
Business Journey

Great leaders are not head-down. They see around corners, shaping
their future, not just reacting to it.

—Roselinde Torres, senior partner
and managing director, BCG[1]

I n the last chapter, we explored how "zooming out" can help a founder CEO
to be aware of where they are in the unfolding story of their enterprise. But
what are the main leadership imperatives for the business journey, and how
do they change along the pathway described in the last chapter?

Now that we have orientated our business, we need a compass to
guide it along that pathway. On the back of the 2018 Value Partnership
research, we developed our "Leadership Compass" to provide some high-
level guidance to CEOs and their teams as they navigate their journey. The
Leadership Compass is a leadership framework that describes the qualities
that a great business requires in six areas (see figure 16.1).

The Leadership Compass (below) points to the *outcomes* of great leadership: a business with a clear sense of direction, an aligned organization, engaged people, and the capabilities to succeed. These fundamentals form the basis for the rest of this section of the book—and represent key facets of the role of a leader. As your business grows, scales, and becomes more sophisticated, these fundamentals will increasingly demand more of your attention as a leader CEO.

Figure 16.1. Image by permission of Value Partnership Ventures Ltd and Value Partnership Ltd. All rights reserved.

I won't go into the details of each Compass point here—they are the subject of the chapters that follow. Each of them requires some careful consideration. Each of them must evolve as the business grows and changes. Each of them brings a cost if neglected. As you consider the framework, you are probably already naturally drawn to some areas and less to others. But they all matter, and they are all linked. A well-designed organization lacking the necessary talent will not succeed. A strategy not directed toward your purpose will take you somewhere else. Leadership has a huge impact on culture that will enable or disable the most beautifully crafted strategy.

Let's take a very high-profile example and a company I know well (and am fond of!), Electronic Arts (EA), one of the world's biggest publishers of computer games, famous for titles such as the *FIFA* (now rebranded as *EA Sports FC*) and the *Battlefield* games series. EA twice had the dubious honor of being named the worst company in America by consumers voting in a Consumerist poll in 2012 and 2013.[2] Too many customers saw EA as a greedy, moneymaking machine, focused more on driving margins than creating good quality products. This impression was reinforced when a number of company insiders spoke anonymously to the press about EA's strategy at the time. The company was under immense pressure from shareholders to grow financial returns, but the more focused EA became on growing profits, the more sales continued to decline.

Winning the worst company award seemed to jolt EA into action. The company needed different *leadership* and a different *culture*. In September 2013, EA appointed Andrew Wilson, an internal appointment, as CEO. Wilson wanted executives to rally behind a code of conduct: Think Players First. That meant making decisions in the best interest of customers/players rather than merely for the company. Wilson changed the way EA was led, changed its culture to be *player-first*, and made decisions that demonstrated he was ready to act in a way consistent with that, such as delaying the launch of a highly anticipated new title, a futuristic war game called *Titanfall*, until the game quality was up to scratch. EA was refocusing on its real purpose: creating awesome games, delivering an exceptional customer experience, and driving innovation.[3]

EA is a stage 6 company based on our framework—a company

showing a readiness to reassess and evolve. A new sense of purpose and a cultural evolution has put the company on a better path thanks to the right kind of leadership. EA illustrates that every company, however big, must constantly adapt in order to thrive. But I'm guessing it's a long way from the challenges that you and your team are facing, at least in terms of scale and maturity.

Navigating Your Business Journey

We have mapped, at a high level, what is required from leadership at each stage of the business journey, from stage 1 to stage 6. The *business journey framework* (see figure 16.2) sits at the confluence of the Compass and the six business growth stages. It's designed to enable you and your team to take a holistic view of where the business is today and *where it needs to be* in order to tackle the particular challenges it faces.

The experience baked into this framework is intended to help you to think systemically about your business, where it is on its growth journey, and the qualities/standards required for continued success. Practically speaking, it should help you to prioritize the critical few things that need attention from a myriad of possibilities.

For example, when we introduced a very purpose-and-values-led founder to the business journey framework, she realized she had assembled a very talented, values-driven workforce, but they were working in a chaotic organization with a distinct lack of strategic focus and performance accountability. It helped her to see that imbalance and to think about what she could do to address it. We collaborated to design and implement a new strategy, a set of purpose-driven OKRs (objectives and key results), and a clear set of roles and accountabilities across her team.

What does your leadership agenda look like? This is not simply about

Navigating Your Business Journey

A map of what is required from leadership at each stage of the business journey. . .

	1. Starting	2. Establishing	3. Growing	4. Leading	5. Maturing	6. Reinventing
Leadership	Founder-led	Add specialists into critical areas	Integrated & Aligned team	Raise standards of performance	Reenergize the team / Deal with complexity & risk / Foster innovation	New external perspectives / Cognitive diversity
Purpose	The "why" is clear	Embed purpose / Make it explicit	Keep purpose center stage	Leverage as a source of competitive advantage / Powerful link to brand	Leverage your heritage / Amplify	Readiness to reassess & evolve / New sense of purpose
Culture	The values are clear	Embed values / Make them explicit	Keep culture center stage	Leverage as a source of competitive advantage / Powerful link to a brand	Leverage your heritage / Revitalize, encourage innovation	Readiness to reassess & evolve / Culture evolution
Strategy	Clear ambition / Path to profitability	Proof of concept / Opportunism / Deepen understanding of markets & customers	Scale up / Specific growth plan	Short- & long-term thinking / Shape the market & regulatory environment	Maximize returns / Make tough strategic choices, e.g., M&A	Pivot & create new focus / Foster new ventures
Organization	Informal, agile / Organic	Clearer roles & minimum process / Embed teamwork	Team of teams / Empowered / Process innovation	Ownership of performance across teams / Manage complexity	Lean management / Encourage experimentation & failure	Appropriate to the stage of business evolution
Talent	Recruit for values *and* capability	Inspire & attract talent to take the business to the next level	Hire & develop for growth / Think strategically about talent	Capitalize on lead position / Develop to retain	Retain talent / Ensure ability to reinvent	Build strategic & change capability

Figure 16.2. Image by permission of Value Partnership Ventures Ltd and Value Partnership Ltd. All rights reserved.

identifying weak points. It is fundamentally about identifying what will help you take the next significant step in pursuit of your business purpose.

Reflections on Navigating Your Business Journey

1. When you consider the business journey framework, what are the "compass points" that need the most attention in your business?

2. What are the few critical things that need addressing for your business to thrive?

3. How can you approach acting on those critical areas in a smart way? (This question will become easier to answer once you have read the rest of Part II The Job of a Leader.)

CHAPTER 17

Finding True North

If you think you are too small to make a difference, try sleeping with a mosquito.

—Dalai Lama XIV, quoting an old African proverb

Purpose is what should guide the journey of your business/enterprise. Clarity of purpose provides a true north for decision-making and creates a powerful glue to unite the team. A genuine purpose is your reason for being and is deeply held. It is your source of shared motivation.

Whatever your business or organization does, it needs to have an aspirational and authentic purpose beyond simply making a profit. Your "why" is bigger than what you do or how you do it. Purpose is your North Star. It guides you throughout the journey your business is on because it represents your raison d'être. If you're true to your purpose, your people and your customers will follow you even when times are hard. If building a business is a marathon, purpose is the fuel you need to keep going; it's the long-term performance engine, as Dutch author Jeroen De Flander calls it.[1]

In chapter 6, we explored *your* purpose, the reason that you founded your business or social enterprise. As I said, that purpose alignment is a principal motivator for *all of us*. The leadership challenge is to align your team or workforce with that purpose. If you do, you will engender high levels of grit, motivation, and health—with significant economic upside.

Purpose can get lost in the day-to-day pressures of running a business. Firefighting the next crisis or dealing with an internal issue can quickly take your eye off the ball. But holding to your purpose will inspire not only the company but also your customers. One study, the 2020 Zeno Strength of Purpose research, asked eight thousand consumers across eight countries about more than seventy-five brands. They found that "global consumers are four to six times more likely to trust, buy, champion, and protect those companies with a strong purpose over those with a weaker one."[2]

TOMS is a for-profit company based in Los Angeles, California. As a shoe manufacturer, TOMS matches every pair of shoes sold with a new pair of shoes for a child in need—this business model is known as the "one-for-one concept." Today, through products such as shoes, eyewear, coffee, and bags, the company provides shoes, sight, water, safe birth, and bullying prevention services to people in need. TOMS is in business to improve lives, and it reports on its impact in detail. Not surprisingly, TOMS is a B Corp. To date, TOMS has given more than fifty million pairs of new shoes to children in need in some seventy developing countries. Accomplishing its charitable goals requires collaborating with more than one hundred NGOs and other nonprofit "giving partners" in these countries.[3]

In 2014, Bain Capital acquired 50 percent of TOMS. Reuters reported that the transaction valued the company at $625 million. Founder Blake Mycoskie retained 50 percent ownership, as well as his role as "Chief Shoe Giver." Mycoskie used half of the proceeds from the sale to start a new fund to support socially minded entrepreneurship, and Bain matched his investment while continuing the company's one-for-one policy. More recently, TOMS has struggled to deal with competitors who started copying not only the company's canvas shoes but also its charitable model. In 2019, its creditors stepped in to provide debt relief and $35 million of new investment to show their commitment to support the future growth of TOMS. While the company continues to donate shoes, its charitable model has evolved. It now says it commits one-third of its net profits toward a giving fund that finances a wide range of philanthropic and social causes. The decline in TOMS revenue shows that being socially conscious does not immunize you from the markets.[4]

Another example of being purpose-led at scale is Patagonia, the apparel company that I mentioned in chapter 12. In an open letter, founder Yvon Chouinard says, "Earth is now our only shareholder." Here's how it works: 100 percent of the company's voting stock transfers to the Patagonia Purpose Trust, created to protect the company's values, and 100 percent of the nonvoting stock is given to the Holdfast Collective, a nonprofit dedicated to fighting the environmental crisis and defending nature. The funding will come from Patagonia; each year, the money they make after reinvesting in the business will be distributed as a dividend to help fight the crisis.

As Nicole Motter, founder and chief strategist at Social Innovation Strategies, says, "Innovative, mission-driven businesses come in many models—and purpose lies at the heart of them all." She has even created a spectrum for us to understand some of the distinctions, based on the degree to which core activities focus on charitable and social causes:

> Entrepreneurial Nonprofit—funded by grants from foundations and donations from the general public

> Non-Nonprofit—exists primarily to address a social issue, funded by investments from foundations, which provide low-cost capital

> Socially Responsible Business—such as a B Corp, funded by traditional angel investments and venture capital

> Give One, Get One/Donate Portion of Proceeds Model—such as TOMS

> Awareness Brand—sells products designed to engage a community and brings awareness to a social issue

> Everything Else—there are many ways that companies can make a difference

In the end, however, as Nicole says, "what matters is that you're creating something meaningful—whatever model or business idea you're considering."[5]

Make no mistake, this is not only about nonprofits and socially conscious enterprises. Straightforward profit-driven businesses can do many powerful, purposeful things that transform the world we live in—if they articulate that purpose and are uncompromising in their pursuit of it.

Reflections on Finding Your True North

1. Have you articulated that purpose so all your key stakeholders can be inspired and informed by it?

2. Are you clear about the operating model for your purpose-led enterprise?

3. Have you ensured that the strategy of the business is directed toward that purpose and not simply giving "lip service" to it?

4. Have you found ways to ensure that impact is real, measurable, and sustainable?

CHAPTER 18

Embedding Purpose

Embedding purpose into your business will help it to stand out, and align it with customers who have the same values.

—Richard Branson[1]

In chapter 17, we said it's up to leaders to figure out how to connect people's work to the higher purpose—because we know that purpose can get lost in the day-to-day pressures of running a business. Employees are searching for meaning in their work but often feel disconnected from the language and presentations leaders make.

Both at work and away from work, all of us seek to fulfill a fundamental human need to belong and contribute. That sense of purpose can be "big P" or "little p." "Big P" is directly linked to the overall purpose of the organization. "Little p" is feeling valued for your individual contribution to the performance of the business, however that is measured.

Both matter. This has been proved through behavioral experiments. Francesca Gino and colleagues from the Harvard Business School carried out an experiment in which employees harvesting tomatoes in California were shown a video explaining how their work had a positive impact in the tomato-processing plant. These employees achieved a 7 percent improvement in productivity relative to the control group that did not watch the video. The Harvard team believes that the positive words from their colleague in the video increased the workers' sense of belonging and therefore their motivation.[2]

A few years ago, Value Partnership won a big leadership development contract with a major French client. At our expense, we took our two support team members with us to meet the client team with whom they would be collaborating. They would be managing the logistics for this client. We wanted them to fully understand the purpose behind the work, build trusting relationships with their French colleagues, and be mindful of the challenges our consultants faced when delivering the program. On the first trip, we introduced them personally to the client and organization. On the second trip, they observed the first workshop. Meeting the client in person gave them the end-to-end understanding of the project, increased connection, and provided a deeper understanding of what success would look like. Their motivation was very high. They gave exceptional support to our consultants and client as they fully appreciated the challenge that they faced.

If you don't hire enough people who believe in your purpose, you'll fall short on motivation and coordination. But as with just about everything in life, you can have too much of a good thing. Hire too many people who are passionate about your purpose, and you'll risk being more vulnerable to "groupthink." You'll end up with evangelists with blind faith in your purpose who never question the side effects or unintended consequences. Perhaps every workplace needs at least a handful of people who *aren't* committed to the organization's purpose. We can count on these people to anticipate any harm the purpose might do—and take action to prevent it.

Leaders need to show up consistently to demonstrate their unwavering commitment to the purpose of their organization. We need to connect what people do day to day to the purpose of the organization ("You are responsible for the customer experience; let's talk about why that has such a central importance to our organization's performance"). Even more powerful, *show* people how their work impacts colleagues, clients, patients, or the environment. Commitment isn't about words. It's about the actions you take that show your commitment and affirm your leadership qualities. If you lead others and don't know what commitment looks like, how can you show others what it means? How can others be committed if they don't know what it looks like?

During the transformation of British Airways in the late 1980s and early 1990s into "The World's Favourite Airline," CEO Colin Marshall demonstrated his personal commitment to the "Putting People First" program. He attended almost all the PPF courses that ran, "setting out his vision for BA and participating in question-and-answer sessions with staff. . . . Each time he flew, he would introduce himself to frontline staff and passengers and discuss their experience with BA. Once, when a queue formed at the launch of a new service, he helped to deliver breakfasts to customers."[3] During the 1990s, British Airways became the world's most profitable airline.

If your company's purpose is just a poster on the wall, you're wasting everyone's time. If you talk about purpose but don't follow through, the results can be devastatingly bad. Dan Cable, an organizational behavior professor at London Business School, says, "Most leaders agree that employees do not 'get' their organizations' purpose. This is because purpose is personal and emotional. It is often managed poorly by transactional leaders who deliver speeches about lofty societal goals rather than helping put employees in direct contact with the people they serve. Purpose can work wonders for employee contributions when leaders start with a personal, authentic, and perpetual approach."[4]

Reflections on Embedding Purpose

1. How well do you connect the purpose of your organization to the work of your team members?

2. Do you help people to make their own connection to that purpose?

3. Are you investing in experiences that directly put people in touch with that purpose and show them what it really means?

4. Is your organizational purpose reflected in the culture of your enterprise?

CHAPTER 19

Building Culture

Culture is a dynamic process of solving human problems and dilemmas.

—Fons Trompenaars, *Riding the Waves of Culture*

When you think about your business and the way people speak and act toward one another and to customers, what do you notice? How do they treat one another? Are they adding value? Are they consistent? Is this the culture you want, or is this simply the culture you have gotten? Is it an accident or by design?

Given the way culture is frequently discussed, a leader could be forgiven for thinking it isn't something that is readily "manageable." Everyone says it's important, but everyone seems to struggle with it. Culture *is* a bit elusive, because much of it is anchored in unspoken behaviors, mindsets, and social patterns.

This is not one of those things that you can give some short-lived attention to and then move on to something else. This is one of those things that requires consistent attention. Given that, the prize better be worth it, right? It absolutely is. It's worth 20 to 30 percent of the differential in corporate performance when compared with "culturally unremarkable" competitors, according to Professor James Heskett in his book *The Culture Cycle*.[1] There aren't many differentiators as powerful as that, and that's why new and experienced CEOs alike are paying significant attention to it.

Our own research, carried out largely in 2018, showed that over half of companies didn't believe their existing culture would support their growth agenda. The right culture engages, retains, and inspires. As one CEO of a digital platform business put it to me, "Strong cultural alignment is the key to pace."

As your company evolves, so will your culture, because solving problems both teaches us and changes us. Founders, for example, are typically concerned in the early days with speed, action, and managing cash. These things are likely to become embedded into the culture of the firm. They also may get diluted as the business grows, other concerns emerge, and new people start getting involved. This is the point at which you need to realize what culture really means for you as the founder CEO—it is how you leverage yourself. You are not scalable, but your culture *is*. It will determine how people think, make decisions, and act when you are *not* present.

As the business begins to mature and the market/technology shifts, the problems change, and the culture must evolve. When I work with businesses at this point in their journey, I sometimes see signs that the culture is no longer serving the business as well as it once did. For example, a video game business, where quality meant taking pride in the detail and authenticity of every aspect of the product, spilled over into an era of live services that made it intensely difficult to deliver at speed and with agility. In developing games as a service, players expect the game to evolve through multiple updates and for their feedback to shape the evolution of the game. Leaders need to be aware of such systemic problems and respond with clear intent or they are unwittingly putting the performance and future of their business at risk.

One of the biggest challenges companies have had to solve in recent times is the impact of the pandemic. You can probably see the way it has influenced the culture of your business—sometimes for better, sometimes for worse. For example, the pandemic massively accelerated change toward flexible working. The nature of collaboration has changed with technology. Social opportunities have been lost because workforces are much more distributed. And yet they can now be more culturally diverse. Teams have pulled together through challenging times and become closer through this experience. The environment for shaping culture has undoubtedly changed, and you need to factor that into your approach to culture. We are perhaps in a new era of culture.

New era or not, culture is an important dimension of your opportunity to establish a precious legacy. Founders can set a culture in motion and imprint values and assumptions that persist for many years. So, when you think about culture, be clear what you really want. Define what great looks like. The answer will depend on the nature of your business (the nature of the problems you need to solve). So, a biotechnology firm delivering innovation through a team of pioneers in multiple scientific disciplines will rightly put a premium on *collaboration*. That leads to one question: What behaviors are critical to live that value? In our leadership consultancy, we place great store on being *true partners* to our clients. This means seeking genuinely authentic relationships, where supporting sometimes means challenging and pushing back.

When trying to define their culture, many organizations confuse *aspirational* values with *core* values. Values do not become core values by placing them in a corporate values statement—that approach is superficial and lacks credibility. Values need to be authentic. And generic value statements such as teamwork, quality, customer satisfaction, and innovation don't set an organization apart from competitors. Patrick Lencioni, in his 2012 book *The Advantage*, distinguishes between core, aspirational, accidental, and what he calls "permission-to-play" values—the latter being minimum behavioral standards such as honesty or integrity.[2] These are table stakes, not real differentiators.

One of my clients, The Chemistry Group, a talent management consultancy based in London, did a brilliant job in defining the authentic culture of their consultancy business around four distinct values:

> People first

> Working in flow

> Science and storytelling

> Love the problem[3]

Each of these values is described through sample behaviors and stories. Together they are an intentional blend of both core and aspirational values that add value to their business. What *you* should seek is a unique culture that *serves your business* and has a direct positive impact on business decisions and performance over time.

Reflections on Building Culture

1. Do you have conviction about the way culture drives business success for your company?

2. Do you have a clear view of the culture you have today, without rose-tinted glasses?

3. Do you have a clear view of the culture you want for the business, and why?

4. Have you involved your team in defining this culture, to secure their ownership and to agree on practical action?

CHAPTER 20

Acting on Culture

Corporate culture is the only sustainable competitive advantage that is completely within the control of the entrepreneur.

—David Cummings, serial entrepreneur[1]

Culture isn't somehow separate; it's part of a system and built for a purpose—it's the way you solve problems dynamically. The late Ed Schein, who was a leading thinker on corporate culture, listed the top three ways in which we can change culture:

> What a leader attends to, measures, rewards, and controls

> How leaders react to critical incidents (do they get defensive, go on the attack, support, blame?)

> Leader role modeling and coaching[2]

All of them are about leadership, which is the single most important factor in shaping culture. Your decisions and day-to-day behavior are actively shaping the culture, for better or for worse. You cast a long shadow. If you do not "live" this culture yourself as CEO, it is "dead on arrival." The upside is that you have a *major* influence. Every day, there are opportunities for you to foster connections with team members, show empathy, and help them to understand and make their contribution to the purpose and performance of the business.

One of the most profound opportunities you have as a leader to influence the culture is in moments of crisis. How you behave in these moments will leave a lasting impression. Your values should guide you in these moments, and if they do, others will see them as a truth.

The late, great Peter Drucker said, "Unless we determine what shall be measured and what the yardstick of measurement in an area will be, the area itself will not be seen."[3] What we measure in business has a profound impact on our team's behavior. If we reward salespeople based on number of leads, we risk creating tons of poor, unqualified leads that take up quality time that should have been spent elsewhere. Notoriously, Wells Fargo Bank massively incentivized the metric of "new accounts," which caused team members to set up thousands of fake accounts, ultimately resulting in major lawsuits and financial impact.

Developing the culture of your organization in an intentional way is not the work of a moment. Think of it like building trust. Trust is built over time through consistent, reliable, high integrity behavior. The moment you breach this pattern, that trust is rapidly destroyed. Developing the culture of your business requires consistent, reliable, high integrity behavior over time. The prize is worth it, though. Alongside an engaging purpose, a distinctive culture can be turned into the conviction you and your people need to provide a competitive advantage.

I was once asked to facilitate a culture meeting for a leadership team— they wanted to shape the culture of their business for the future. The thing is, they had a set of values articulated already, embedded in their corporate communications. I asked the team about the existing values at the start of the meeting; they couldn't name a single one—awkward but necessary pain for them. If you are serious about culture, you need serious conviction about what it is, why it matters, and how you live it every day. This team was also a low-performing team, riddled with mistrust. You can't get genuine consensus about a desired culture if the team is not a team. And if the leadership team is not functioning well, the culture will also not meet expectations.

There are many different third-party tools for measuring and tracking culture, such as Culture Amp®, the people and culture platform. For something as seemingly intangible as culture, increasing its measurability is vital. As well as using some powerful, well-researched benchmark questions, you also can design your own value-specific items. Alongside this data-driven approach, you can do much simpler things. Try the David Cummings "Hallway Test" (which you can adapt to Zoom, of course):

> "Independently stop ten employees in the hallway.

> Ask each employee to write down the company values.

> Compare the answers to the actual core values.

> Assess the percentage right and grade it on a typical letter scale."[4]

Whatever data you capture, it's only valuable if you act on it. Show your team members that you value their feedback and show them how serious you are about strengthening the culture and living the values through action. Engage and involve them.

Once you know your desired company culture, you need to build the invisible scaffolding for that culture to prosper. That scaffolding consists of the office environment, the technology you use, habits and routines, symbols, and social and community activities. You are creating the environment within which your preferred culture will prosper. Here's a simple example: If you want to foster learning, organize regular learning activities every month for and with your team. In this way a routine reinforces the desired culture and shows your commitment to it.

As you grow the business, there will come a point when you need to ramp up hiring in order to scale the business. This is a pivotal moment for founders if they want to sustain or actively shape the culture of their business. Every person you hire who does not share your values will divert your culture away from its core values. So, recruit for values, as well as the capability to take the business to the next level. Ask the right questions to elicit potential employees' values.

Finally, let's make sure that people realize that culture matters when "the chips are down." Be clear about what you will *not* tolerate. Values are something you stand for. If you see behavior that is inconsistent with the values, you must call it out if you want to be taken seriously on this. At Netflix, they are clear—"brilliant jerks" will not be tolerated.[5] The cost to effective teamwork is too high. The wrong people will undermine trust, create unnecessary anxiety in other employees, and reduce motivation. Accommodating them means losing others, expensively.

Reflections on Acting on Culture

1. Have you articulated a strong, clear, distinctive set of values and behaviors that truly serve your business?

2. What is your plan for ensuring this culture is in place?

3. How are you going to measure and manage progress in this area?

4. Do you personally role model these values and behaviors consistently?

5. How are you going to create an environment within which your preferred culture will flourish?

6. Do you actively consider culture when people decisions are made?

CHAPTER 21

Setting Strategy

Without strategy, execution is aimless. Without execution, strategy is useless.

—Morris Chang, businessman

This is a big topic. The next one thousand words will not scratch the surface of the thousands of books on this subject. But it might help you to approach it with the right mindset and questions.

No matter how unpredictable the business environment you inhabit, every business needs a longer-term milestone (vision) and a map for getting there (strategy). This requirement becomes particularly critical at the point of more rapid growth (stage 3 in the business journey referenced in chapter 15) because of the need to engage a growing number of people in the delivery of that strategy.

I have met more than a few founders who avoid setting out their vision, goals, and strategy, arguing they want to remain open-minded and adaptive in a disruptive world. At the risk of sounding a bit bossy, this is a mistake. Inexperienced leaders, fearful of falling short or making a strategic mistake, can be tempted to avoid making an explicit commitment to a particular set of outcomes. Founders need to be much more intentional than that. Strategy involves focus and, therefore, choice. Focus compounds faster than money. For example, a choice to move into mobile gaming because that is where the growth rate is highest. Or a choice to diversify your product offerings, or to focus on the delivery of the core offering.

UCLA management professor Richard Rumelt has written eloquently about the perils of what he calls "bad strategy."[1] In short, the perils are listed here:

> Failure to face the problem (coming up with a wish list instead)

> Mistaking goals for strategy (setting higher targets with no obvious leverage point)

> Bad strategic objectives (a long list of actions instead)

> Fluff (superficial abstractions like being "customer-centric")

One of my clients, a mobile gaming company, recently asked me to facilitate their strategy meeting. They faced several challenges:

> A falling off in organic growth due to a weak economy

> Having a substantial cost base in anticipation of growth

> Geopolitical risk impacting on the funding available for acquisitions

> Technology change making it harder to track users

The test of their strategy had to be the following: Does it tackle these challenges effectively? And does it keep the company on the path toward their vision/purpose? Strategy has to face the challenges honestly and provide a coherent approach to tackling them.

An example of this is SpaceX, founded in 2002 to revolutionize space technology, with the ultimate goal of enabling people to live on other planets. Perhaps the biggest challenge they face is the enormous cost. Reusability allows SpaceX to re-fly the most expensive parts of the rocket, which in turn drives down the cost of space access. Falcon 9 is the world's first orbital class reusable rocket. Elon Musk identified and solved what Richard Rumelt describes as the "crux," the decisive challenge.

A recurrent challenge with strategy setting is securing the support of your investors. I have seen all too often short-term performance pressure from investors that drives short-term decision-making by leaders. The founder and their team need to muster enough confidence and clarity to avoid overpromising and under-delivering. To create the breathing space within which they can deliver real progress and change, leaders need a credible strategic story and a reputation for delivering on promises that is hard-won. These come from an assertive confidence, not just a desire to please. You need to earn the right to be trusted to deliver over time.

Execution is often where strategies flop, something I explore in the next chapter. You can greatly reduce some of the problems of execution by involving the right people in the development of the strategy. The "right people" are those who will be critical and accountable for its successful execution. Who are those people in your organization? Their engagement leads to understanding and ownership. Ownership leads to accountability and action. So, don't do strategy in secret, announce it, and expect excitement and committed action. Instead, run a workshop; open your mind to the best ideas. Let the process breathe. Having defined your strategy, you need to switch gears. The listening and discussion pivots into conviction and action.

Involvement does not mean decisions have to be made by consensus—or by majority opinion. Do not seek to avoid conflict in favor of group harmony. Conflict is *helpful* in decision-making (see chapter 29) because it can uncover the hidden assumptions and data that lead people to make *less* well-informed decisions. Lack of healthy conflict ensures lack of commitment. Opinions need to be aired properly in passionate and open debate to get buy-in and commitment to group decisions. Clear and specific resolutions and calls to action result instead of ambiguity. Ensure the discussions consist of "substance" rather than "theater" and that the most difficult issues are on the table. An experienced facilitator might be useful to make sure that happens. As a leader, you need to encourage diverse thoughts and opinions around the table to discover more innovative solutions. One thing that you have every right to hold on to as a founder leader is the vision. As Jeff Bezos said, "We are stubborn on vision. We are flexible on details."[2]

Reflections on Setting Strategy

1. Are you involving the right people in an authentic conversation about the challenges and how to address them?

2. How clear are you and your team about the big challenges that your enterprise faces?

3. Have you identified a coherent approach for tackling those issues?

4. Have you put your purpose at the core of your strategy?

5. Are you ready to put your judgment on the line, make hard choices, and focus on what really matters?

CHAPTER 22

Executing Strategy

Seventy percent of strategic failures are due to poor execution of leadership. It's rarely for lack of smarts or vision.

—Ram Charan, author and business advisor[1]

The challenge of developing a strategy is often dwarfed by the difficulties of strategy execution. Why is this the case? Why is it so hard to implement a strategy? Many founders know, broadly speaking, what they want to do. It is the doing itself that confounds them.

A quote often attributed to Bill Gates is, "Most people overestimate what they can achieve in a year and underestimate what they can achieve in ten years." This resonates strongly with my experience of working with leadership teams in companies both big and small. There is a temptation to take on way too much (and maybe avoid making difficult choices) in year one, and by the end of that, the hard work of seeing significant changes through has become readily apparent. The inconvenient and annoying truth is that anything important tends to happen slowly.

In the age of "unicorn" companies—transforming the possibilities in an industry in double-quick time—it is becoming unfashionable to look at the hard yards of progressive transformation and continuous improvement. Hilton took about one hundred years to create a business that has the capacity of seven hundred thousand rooms. Airbnb has a capacity of one million rooms, a feat that has taken less than six years. Remember, however, that the Airbnbs of this world are set up for "new."

It matters greatly to the majority of businesses to master more progressive change. If you can get 10 percent better every year, then you will be about twice as good in less than eight years. This is the mathematics of sustainable organizational change. Not quite as exciting as the world of unicorns, is it? It's real, though, and over time, it makes a massive difference. It takes applying ideas to the world, feeling them out, redoubling yourself, and trying again. It's not giving up when you forget or fail. It is through the process of refinement that we learn new habits and ideas.

Strategic execution and change require forming strong relationships that can survive and benefit from challenging conversations. It requires building a diverse and talented team. Creating a positive culture. Being aware of, understanding, and responding to external influences. It may require being prepared to stop doing something when we're not getting the results we wanted, admitting that we got it wrong, and changing course. Very human traits, rooted in vulnerability.

Both in my own business, and in the businesses that I have coached, I see the constant learning and adaptation that is necessary to unlock growth and change. Progress is uneven, talent comes and goes, markets change, the economy tanks. It is more sailboat than speedboat: Constant "tacking" is required to reach your destination, sometimes in very stormy seas. Strategy, therefore, should not be seen as an annual event—more as a process of learning. If we learn faster or better than our competitors, we will have a competitive advantage.

I have vivid recollections of being part of the Ericsson UK team in the 1990s, at the point when the business required a transformation from a predominantly fixed network to a mobile network business. We had a clear vision of where we needed to get to, but the size of the task was huge. The mistake we made initially was to kick-start too many projects, with what we later realized was a distinct lack of focus and coordination. We reviewed progress as a team three months in and discovered we were barely moving, despite the whirlwind of activity. We mapped it all out on a huge whiteboard and discovered the sheer extent of the agenda and, less obvious, the overreliance on a few key people to make critical things happen. We reduced the project list by 80 percent and stage-managed the road map to allow better talent allocation decisions. And we immediately had momentum. "The weakest living creature, by concentrating his powers on a single object, can accomplish something: the strongest, by dispersing his over many, may fail to accomplish anything," observed the Scottish historian and philosopher Thomas Carlyle.[2]

Ultimately, as described by Chris McChesney, Sean Covey, and Jim Huling in their book, *The 4 Disciplines of Execution*, a strategy needs to be translated into a compelling road map that is focused on the "wildly important," enables us to act on the lead measures, tells us at a glance where we stand, and creates a "cadence of accountability."[3] *Compelling* means that those people who have to deliver it believe in it; they know why it's worth going the extra mile for. Getting the key measures right is an essential precondition for managing the progress of strategy execution as a team. Outcome measures like profitability matter, but the best way of delivering profit is by focusing on lead measures, the drivers of profitability, which means understanding the market, the customer delivery required, and the organization that will make it happen. With this, the team can decide when and how to course correct as it steers the organization through changing market conditions.

When it comes to execution, setting goals, tracking progress, and adapting can be aided by establishing a clear, systemic methodology. Objectives and key results (OKRs) is a useful goal-setting framework used by individuals, teams, and organizations to define measurable goals and track their outcomes. The development of OKRs is generally attributed to Andrew Grove, who introduced the approach to Intel in the 1970s. The important thing is not necessarily using this method, but defining goals and tracking progress in a way that works for you and your enterprise.

Reflections on Executing Strategy

1. Have you done the work during your strategy setting so you and your team have powerful conviction behind your action agenda?

2. Have you made clear choices so your two to three objectives and key results are laser-focused?

3. Have you established a systemic methodology for goal setting and a compelling scorecard that tells everyone where they stand?

4. Regular meetings are essential to track progress, solve problems, and learn/pivot. Have you established that cadence of accountability?

CHAPTER 23

Designing the Organization

*No one pretends that democracy is perfect or all-wise. Indeed, it has
been said that democracy is the worst form of Government except for
all those other forms that have been tried from time to time.*

—Winston Churchill, November 11, 1947

The same can be said for the design of organizations: They all have their flaws. It is about finding the one that works best. Delivering on your purpose, vision, and strategy requires an organization designed with your purpose, vision, and strategy in mind.

During the early stages in the life of a business, everyone fits into one room, and most things can be dealt with in an informal and organic way. But once you start growing and running into specialized or complex problems, the initial team needs reinforcing. Specialists like a finance person are brought in, and functional teams emerge. From this point on, the organization requires constant adaption to enable growth.

When a startup has only one product, functional grouping typically makes sense. As the startup grows and expands its product portfolio, it either stays functional or evolves into a product or hybrid organization. Do you group people from the same function under one manager, with the benefit of subject matter added value (e.g., user acquisition specialists reporting to a UA lead), or do you group people working on the same product under one product lead, with the benefit of product/market focus? Or do you have a hybrid model with some roles centralized and others decentralized? When venture-backed startups enter a fast-growth phase, they generally hire rapidly. As a result, reporting structures can become blurred and levels can proliferate—the design becomes distorted and decision-making authority unclear. One telltale sign is the new hires not knowing what is expected of them, to whom they can turn for help, and how they can grow within the organization. This is why organizational design matters during every phase of the organization's life, but especially during scale-up.

Miniclip has pivoted from a functional leadership structure, which was crucial in transforming the company into a mobile gaming business, into a business unit structure in which product and brand teams "own" their businesses. Acquisitions can be integrated more easily into the growing group, and dependencies are kept to a minimum. It achieves what Amazon executives Colin Bryar and Bill Carr describe in their book, *Working Backwards*, as the principle of separable, single-threaded leadership—when a leader or dedicated team assumes clear, unambiguous ownership of a single outcome with minimum reliance or impact on others. The hard-won insight at Amazon was that cross-team communication didn't need refinement—it needed elimination.[1]

If we look wider, traditional structures in which the business is led from the top by the CEO and blueprinted into functional departments are gradually disappearing and being replaced by more fluid networks of interaction. Technology firms that are using agile software development methodologies have accelerated this innovation. Take Spotify: It uses squads, tribes, alliances, and guilds to organize its business. Spotify has largely succeeded in maintaining an agile mindset and principles without sacrificing accountability. It enables innovation while keeping the benefits of repeatability, and it creates alignment without excessive control. Its lessons apply to many companies, not just technology companies.

And on a larger scale, as first described by Gareth Morgan in his writing, we see the emergence of loosely coupled networks, ideal for conditions requiring flexibility, innovation, and change.[2] Control is achieved through measuring results. The team at the center steers the whole enterprise, strategy, tactics, and resource flows. Membership of the network is in flux. Relationships are based on knowledge and competence, not authority, and information networks provide a platform for instant, informal, and unstructured communication.

It might help to think about the work of an organization in three parts:

> Growth investment (leadership, strategy, talent, investment)

> Customer delivery (product, operations, sales, customer support)

> Support infrastructure (finance, HR, IT)

Invest in the first category, manage the performance of the second, and minimize the cost/maximize the value of the third. As founder CEO, you should consider whether your organization structure is enabling you to focus your attention on the first category, because that's where your job lies.

Whatever design you choose, remember that it's *how people behave* within that framework that will determine the outcome, rather than the structure itself. Almost no business operates as the organization chart suggests. People find ways to make it work, often in spite of the structure. That's OK. What counts is whether the structure *works*.

Organization design is about unlocking and enabling growth and agility—creating a team of teams that can work together to deliver your purpose and strategy. As coach and author Jamil Qureshi has pointed out, we live in an era where "communities are outperforming bureaucracies and hierarchies."[3] So, be prepared to create accountable teams and empower them to deliver. If you have a healthy culture and talented team, this shouldn't fill you with dread. Spotify strives to offer a high degree of autonomy without suffering from a lack of alignment. Henrik Kniberg, an agile coach at Spotify, puts it this way: "The stronger alignment we have, the more autonomy we can afford to grant."[4] In other words, the more you engender shared purpose, vision, culture, and strategy, the more you can afford to trust your teams to deliver.

Reflections on Designing the Organization

1. As the business grows, are you consciously standing back to evaluate whether the organization structure is meeting the needs of the business (its purpose, vision, and strategy)?

2. From time to time, are you checking in with team members about how the structure is working and what would make it work better? Not just your managers, but also the people who deal directly with products and customers.

3. Have you created strong purpose/vision alignment across your teams so you can trust teams to work autonomously and use their talent to best effect?

4. As CEO, does your structural design enable you to focus your energy on growth rather than operations?

CHAPTER 24

Managing Talent

The true measure of a successful leader is their ability to discover the hidden talent in those they lead and challenge them to achieve greatness.

—Henry Ford, industrialist

To fuel growth, you need talent. Attracting the right people is just the beginning. Retaining and growing them requires even more effort. And every business has talent just waiting to be unleashed to take it forward.

Who are the "right people" for your business? They will care about your purpose, share your values, and bring energy, potential, and capabilities the business needs. Together, they will provide a sufficiently diverse team to ensure the business can balance innovation with stability, strategic thinking with execution excellence. And you will get the best from them only if you create a context in which they can perform and thrive.

Developing your talent in line with your growth plans is core to growing a successful business. Thinking and acting strategically about talent is one of the hallmarks of great leadership. You need to develop talent before rather than when you need it. Even if you "buy" talent, it takes time for them to become integrated and effective. A number of different businesses I've worked with could see the emerging need for general management talent as the business grew and needed to decentralize. The impact on future performance of acting early to both identify and prepare talent for such roles was economically very significant. A failure to do so also led to economically significant consequences.

I have seen many situations where talent held a business back or unlocked rapid progress. One client who went on to seriously scale initially was held back by two things. One was a lack of strategic focus. The other was a senior team made up of the founder's friends and connections, brought in because they were known and trusted. The truth was, that team lacked what it would take to transform the business and drive growth. So, the CEO and I developed a plan to systematically develop the team through a combination of hires, departures, and coaching. That, in combination with strategic focus, rapidly transformed the performance and growth prospects of the company. It was hard for the founder to have some of those conversations, but done with compassion, it was ultimately the right thing for everyone.

In a totally different setting, an early-stage insurtech client wanted to grow its business in the German market. They hired a salesman with apparently relevant industry and corporate experience. Unfortunately, he was a poor cultural fit and a natural strategist who was weak at implementation. Relationships were being built, but leads were not converted—there was a lack of pace. This took time to become visible because he worked in relative isolation away from the main office. Precious time and money were lost discovering they had made a poor hire. (In chapter 34 we explore what it takes to hire well.)

Roger Philby, founder and CEO of The Chemistry Group, says that we should move from a *scarcity* mindset to an *abundance* mindset about talent. We should stop thinking of talent as being about exceptional people and start thinking about how we can find the talent in everyone. As he puts it, the purpose of The Chemistry Group is to give everybody the opportunity to be brilliant at work. Roger says, "We believe the world is measuring talent wrong by putting all their emphasis on academic ability and experience and neither of these two things in our measurement in the last nine years are ever the most important predictors of performance."

The Chemistry Group uses a model of talent:

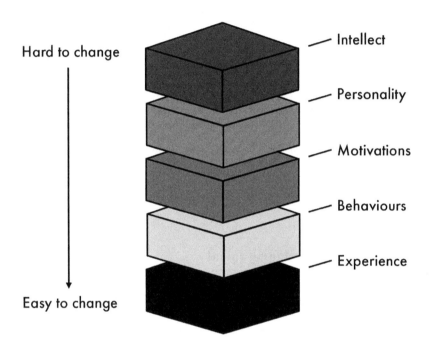

Figure 24.1. Image by permission of The Chemistry Group. All rights reserved.

The higher up in the stack, the harder it is to change. Behavior is changeable, as is experience. The "right people" is something you need to define. Even if you know what to do, whether you do it or not is driven by your values and your motivation. If those things resonate with the environment and culture you are in, you will feel "at home" and be able to perform. It's predictable to a large degree.

Everything I wrote about understanding and working on yourself (see chapters 1 and 5) also applies to each person who works for you. We all share a fundamental psychological need to develop our competence, to grow personally and professionally. Developing our potential is a core motivator, especially (but not only) for young people. As leaders, we have a responsibility to invest in our teams—it benefits both us and our businesses.

A 2016 Oxford Economics study sponsored by SAP showed that high-performing companies invest in training, mentoring, and developing their talent. The study's findings are based on feedback from over forty-one hundred executives and employees worldwide. They found a direct correlation between high-performing companies—which they called "Digital Winners"—and certain practices. When it came to talent management, the "Winners" had more mature strategies and programs for hiring skilled talent (85 percent versus 64 percent). And 84 percent of respondents of "Winners" expect their leaders to develop talent and reward them for doing so. Perhaps not surprisingly, their employees are happier and more loyal, routinely going beyond minimum job requirements.[1]

Reflections on Managing Talent

1. Have you figured out "what great looks like" for talent in your business?

2. Do you assess for values, motivation, and impact, not just for experience and academic achievement?

3. Are you thinking ahead to what your business will need to drive your growth plans?

4. Do you invest energy and money to develop *all* the talent in your business?

PART III

TACTICAL CHALLENGES

CHAPTER 25

Leading Change and Innovation

We must learn what customers really want, not what they say they want or what we think they should want.

—Eric Ries, *The Lean Startup*

Innovation is the lifeblood of growing companies. But to foster it on a sustainable and relevant basis, we need to be intentional about our approach.

The journey of a growing business demands constant change and adaptation, and it's the role of the founder CEO to lead that change. Management thinker Peter Drucker argued in his book *Management Challenges for the 21st Century* that unless an organization sees that its task is to lead change—it will not survive.[1] Many founders can attest to that. Innovation helps you to grow your business, stand out from competitors, meet customer needs, and attract the best talent. The question is how to meet that need for innovation. I argue that we need to put in place the means for innovation to ensure it doesn't overly depend on the founder's original thinking.

Change and innovation happen out of both choice and necessity. The COVID-19 pandemic forced many companies to find new products, services, supply chains, and ways of working—companies had to embrace nondiscretionary innovation. One UK food distributor saw its traditional business serving restaurants and institutions rapidly decline, almost overnight, so it implemented a direct-to-consumer food delivery business in less than two weeks, delivered via an easy-to-use mobile app. It's amazing what you can achieve out of necessity!

Another example of nondiscretionary innovation is when a Pakistan-based motorbike ride-hailing business showing strong growth had to fight to compete in a market with no significant barriers to entry and rapidly emerging competition. The company's founder CEO determined that building a powerful ride-hailing network was not enough; the business needed to exploit its growing network in areas like grocery delivery and distribution, innovating and finding ways to use their app to diversify the business. The business strategy needed to be discriminating about identifying the most attractive sectors through customer/market research *and* secure the talent/capital to achieve a breakthrough in those sectors. For innovation to happen, we need to build the capability to both deliver and measure results. This story shows us some important things about innovation:

> Make innovation a part of your strategy, with a clear understanding of the contribution it makes to achieving your vision and purpose.

> Spend substantial time immersing yourself in the marketplace that your company occupies and be astutely aware of your target audience.

> Prove product-market fit with a minimum viable product before investing more heavily.

> Successful innovation is about curating and implementing innovations to drive success and growth. Investment and a solid execution plan need to be in place to make this happen.

The ride-hailing business found the most success when it focused on the needs and wants of customers that they *already knew* rather than building new verticals that required a different or new customer base. A leader in the video gaming sector, for example, learned that the new product they were building demanded *too much* innovation from the team, and it proved to be an expensive financial disappointment. Simply put, they bit off more than they could chew.

Technology is now central to most innovation. Eli Bressert, founder and CEO of tech-first travel company Origin, is demonstrating that artificial intelligence (AI) and machine learning (ML) are powerful enablers for the future of high-touch services such as travel. We instinctively think of high-touch services as unscalable. Bressert's company is leading the creation of what he calls human-in-the-loop systems—in other words, a service or product that leverages the best of machines *and* human agents in one system. Origin designs luxury travel itineraries personalized by "AI-super-powered" travel curators. These individuals can focus 95 percent of their time on crafting bespoke experiences, while AI and ML handle the complexities of scheduling, pricing, and planning according to customer preference. As a result, Origin delivers exceptional travel experiences at scale.

Innovation is typically *in the nature* of the founders of growing companies and is a choice that underpins the potential of their enterprise. Many founders are Game Changers (see The GC Index® in chapter 5) who instinctively generate ideas and new possibilities. They need creative freedom and expression—without which the business may not have existed in the first place. This very drive needs to be complemented with other strengths in order to not only create new ideas but also execute them well. This is where the need for a diverse team (see chapter 38) comes into play.

We need purpose-driven action for original ideas to bear fruit. Teams must learn to temper their desire for innovation—for example, when the business has the imperative to scale and when focus is a higher priority than raw innovation.

The following are key to building a strong capacity for innovation:

> Bake innovation capability into the leadership team. Curate a diverse team with that potential. Trust, diversity, and inclusion are essential for innovation—these are foundation stones for a high-performing team.

> Create a healthy, curious, and innovative culture, not one plagued by a fear of failure. In a psychologically safe environment, employees can use their higher capacity for social engagement, innovation, creativity, and ambition.

> Set up the structure of the organization to facilitate innovation (see the Spotify example in chapter 23).

> Innovation requires investment—it needs organization and focused resources. It requires not just money but also time for people to invest in future possibilities and take risks.

Reflections on Leading Change and Innovation

1. Is innovation a part of your strategy? Where does it matter most for your organization to achieve its purpose?

2. Are you close to your customers and marketplace? Do you act on this understanding, test new products early, and capture insightful business intelligence about what is and isn't working?

3. Do you put the talent and capital in place to drive innovation?

4. Do you have an execution plan to translate ideas into action and results?

5. Are you building a diverse team to drive innovation?

6. Does the culture of your organization make risk-taking and failure "safe"?

7. Is innovation accountability clear in your organization? Do you have measures in place to assess the results of innovation?

CHAPTER 26

Defining Success

Begin with the end in mind.

—Stephen R. Covey,
The 7 Habits of Highly Effective People

How do you know if you have been successful? You don't if you haven't defined what success means. You may have a feeling about it, but is that enough? It lacks a bit of accountability, doesn't it? It's like saying, "Let's just see what happens." If you aim for nothing, you'll hit it every time.

Some of my early work with founder CEOs made me mindful that in some cases, there was a reluctance to commit to a specific goal or goals. Underneath that reluctance was a fear of failure and the loss of face that comes with it. It was expressed as "the market is so uncertain it's really hard to know what is achievable," or something along those lines. But the truth is, not hitting goals isn't failure; it's a lesson learned. Failure is the cost of inaction sometimes. And setting the right goals actually makes all the difference.

Defining success makes you more *accountable*. Sharing that commitment with others *increases* that sense of accountability. The *process* of defining success helps you in surprising ways, too. But it has to be the *right* definition to drive the right decisions and actions.

Why is all this true? In behavioral economics, pre-committing to a goal is one of the most frequently applied behavioral devices to achieve positive change. Committing to a specific future action—for example, staying healthy by practicing yoga at a particular time (three sessions per week on Tuesdays, Thursdays, and Saturdays)—tends to better motivate action, while also reducing procrastination.

In fact, it's generally easier to see this in sports where measurement is second nature. Over five years ago, I set a goal for myself: running a marathon. I also wanted to run it in under a specific time. Making that commitment, sharing it with others, and training consistently to be able to run 26.2 miles enabled me to run the distance. But setting a specific time didn't work out for me. It was my first marathon, and I had no benchmark. I missed my mark and found it hard to shake off the feeling that I had, on some level, failed. That makes no sense at all, given what I had achieved. Better to have focused on running the distance, looking after myself, and enjoying the experience. I set the wrong definition of success.

The time in which you finish a marathon is the equivalent of setting profitability as the goal for a business—it's an outcome, not the purpose. It sometimes leads to the wrong behavior. Cutting costs can boost profits now but leave the business unable to perform next year. One of the reasons leadership is tricky is that the answer doesn't lie in a spreadsheet.

Let's explore a business example when defining success well can really lead to positive change. Many companies are trying to work out how to handle flexible working post-pandemic. What is the right solution for your business—back to working in the office, hybrid, virtual, or fully flexible? It's pretty clear that the right solution for one company is not necessarily the right solution for another. So, how do we get to a "good" answer?

A great first step is to get the senior people in your business agreeing on what success would look like. In one client's company, some managers felt office working was key, while others saw no problem with the "new normal" of working from home with occasional office time. To get aligned on a plan, they defined success together. In this case, the answer was a combination of factors:

> Net positive impact on productivity

> Retention of critical talent

> Impact on ability to recruit in key roles

> Impact on employee engagement scores

> Impact on employee health

> Impact on the desired culture

This shared understanding drove alignment, measurement, and ownership of decisions/action and avoided decisions based either on dated ideas or the latest trend without testing its relevance to their particular business. You can see why the process of defining success (as a management team) led to better decisions/actions than would otherwise have been the case. Everyone involved had more conviction about what to do—because they understood the "why."

We do need to be aware of the problem dynamics when we try to define success. Take the nightmare scenario of aiming to reduce your headcount to put your business in better shape during a slow or shrinking economy. If you define success in cost reduction terms alone, you will fail to see the trap in front of you. The trap is that layoffs can cause employees to feel they've lost control. A 2002 study by Magnus Sverke and Johnny Hellgren of Stockholm University and Katharina Näswall of the University of Canterbury found that after a layoff, survivors experienced a 41 percent decline in job satisfaction, a 36 percent decline in organizational commitment, and a 20 percent decline in job performance.[1] You might want to broaden your success criteria to incorporate attention to these areas, not simply the things you can measure on a set of accounts.

It's not an accident that "what would success look like?" is one of the first questions a coach will ask you, followed by an exploration of the current reality, the options, and a commitment to action. Describe the outcome—paint as specific a picture as possible of how things would be if you have taken a big step forward. All sorts of ideas will likely be triggered by this thought process.

Whenever you are faced with a complex problem, start by defining success. Trust me, it will really help. And it will make success not only clearer, but also much more likely.

Reflections on Defining Success

1. Have you set clear goals for your venture over the next period? Did you also involve your team to enable collective ownership of those goals?

2. Are you confident that your definition of success will drive the right kind of actions and behaviors? The right kind of actions and behaviors are those that are aligned with your purpose (your "why") and your strategy (the "how").

3. Is your definition of success driving alignment, measurement, and ownership of decisions/action? Are you making progress toward your definition of success?

CHAPTER 27

Listening to Others

Listening is a magnetic force.

—Karl Menninger, psychiatrist

You don't know enough on your own; you really don't. You have hired smart people. They bring knowledge, skills, customer experience, all sorts of valuable things that can help you make better decisions. Founders also typically find themselves surrounded by other, more experienced founders, successful businesspeople, investors, and others who have a lot of wisdom to offer. Listen to them. I could stop right there—that's the main message of this chapter. But there is a bit more to say.

Many people listen, as Stephen Covey put it, with the intent to reply rather than the intent to understand. That's not *really* listening. In Redland, a British building materials company later acquired by Lafarge, they used to say Redland managers don't listen; they reload. Foolishly, it was a badge of pride.

About 85 percent of what we know we have learned through listening, but we generally listen at a 25 percent comprehension rate. It makes little sense.

So, what gets in the way of us listening? I think there are a few things in the case of founders. Consider which might apply to you:

> We are so focused and confident about our vision that we refuse to believe feedback to the contrary. We just want validation really. Just tell us our idea is brilliant, please!

> We are afraid of failure. It's tempting to shut out things that make us feel at risk.

> We don't trust others' motives for some reason. "She's just saying that because she wants to sell me something," for example.

> What someone is saying is inconvenient. And we can't face the potential consequences of it. It would require undoing a lot of hard work . . .

> We think they are just telling us what we want to hear, so we don't trust it.

I could go on.

Whatever the nature of the business you are trying to build, you need a product/service offering that solves a genuine problem. And that problem needs to be significant enough, urgent enough, or frequent enough for people to justify forking out some cash for it.

But many founders don't fall in love with the problem they're trying to solve. They fall in love with their solution. They stop listening to critical feedback. They reach out to those who will confirm their biases, and they only speak to those who will validate their assumptions. And guess what? Their product gets better and better at solving a problem that doesn't exist. Estimates show that nearly half of business failures are caused by "misreading market demand."[1] Smart founders want to find out if their product idea is no good as fast as possible. That's why we build a *minimum viable product*. And that's why, if failure it must be, we want to *fail fast*.

Experienced founders are open to feedback and constructive criticism. Listening does not mean you have to agree with or act on everything you hear. Over time, you learn to recognize good advice when you hear it. You learn who to listen to and who not to listen to. Above all else, it's important to know how to put good advice into context.

A good friend, ex-founder, and now venture capitalist looks back on his first venture. It was a women and girls' sports apparel business, and it could have become Lululemon but never made it. Bottom line, he feels that his team, including himself, wasn't good enough. Others told him, and he probably knew it deep down, but he persisted nevertheless. He also reflects that if he had set stronger milestones for progress ("failure points") and held himself and his team accountable to them, it would have been more obvious where they stood and what changes he needed to make as a result. Small failures that enabled course correction perhaps would have led to ultimate success. Instead, one big failure was the outcome.

Great listeners practice something called *active listening*. If you have a great coach, you will have experienced this with them. Active listening was first used in counseling and conflict resolution. When it's done right, active listening—fully listening to the speaker and providing verbal and nonverbal feedback—can help you to draw people out, avoid misunderstandings, foster workplace collaboration, settle disagreements, and gain people's trust. Those who do genuinely listen to their employees are in a much better position to lead the increasingly diverse and multigenerational workforce.

Listening well to your team gives you many benefits:

> Access to knowledge and perspectives that increase your leadership capacity

> A platform for empathy that creates a work environment of trust

> Deeper understanding of the needs of your clients

> Knowledge and insights into the day-to-day reality of your employees and an opportunity to support them

A couple of decades ago, I was working in Paris with a very senior person in the French industrial company Lafarge. He showed me a gift his team had given him, a bell. I asked him what the present was for. He smiled ruefully. No ordinary bell, it was a Zen bell. The closed shape and high weight of this bell make for a concentrated and long-lasting sound. The team was giving him feedback. They wanted him to ring the bell and wait for the sound to die out before responding to an idea or insight from them. They wanted him to really listen and consider what they had to say.

Reflections on Listening to Others

1. Do you *really* listen to the people around you, both inside and outside the business?

2. Can you determine wherein lies real wisdom, rooted in relevant experience? If so, do you place enough weight on that wisdom?

3. Are your listening skills and habits good enough to de-risk your business?

4. Are you listening actively enough to build strong relationships with your employees and customers?

CHAPTER 28

Finding Conviction

Have the courage of your convictions once you have made your decision.

—**Walter Schloss,** legendary Wall Street investor

The Walter Schloss quote applies to leadership, too. But we need to balance that against another sentiment. As Friedrich Nietzsche once said, "A very popular error: having the courage of one's convictions; rather it is a matter of having the courage for an attack on one's convictions."[1] Our convictions *should* stand up to scrutiny, and we should be prepared for that. But once a leader has heard everyone around them, they will ultimately have to decide, either singularly or collaboratively. Even not deciding is still a decision. And then they need to back themselves, or implementation will be halfhearted and may ultimately lack the necessary grit.

Conviction is powerful stuff. It breeds conviction in others, and it's a great trait for a leader to have. It isn't easy to demonstrate conviction in a world plagued with uncertainty—in fact, we know that as uncertainty increases, the brain shifts control over to the limbic system, the place where emotions such as fear are generated. It's not what we want in a business context, and it's a reaction that inhibits us from making choices in the absence of certainty. Perhaps it's a defining quality of a great entrepreneur or leader—the courage of your convictions even in the face of uncertainty. That clarity enables the rest of the team to move ahead and act with confidence.

Conviction works in all areas of life, of course. I ended up on the starting line of my first London Marathon in 2017. I had done the training, but I was still anxious. *What will happen to me after twenty miles?* I wondered. You never run farther than that in training; it takes too much out of you and requires lengthy recovery. Runners typically run out of glycogen (stored energy) after nineteen to twenty miles. As you enter the last six miles of a marathon, your body is very low on carbohydrates and must turn to fat reserves to keep going. That is more painful and is a big concern for a first-time marathoner. Uncertainty and fear make a marathon a big test. I passed this test, but only just. Two years later I ran my second London Marathon. This time, I had conviction on my side. Why? Because it was no longer an unknown. I trained better, fueled better, and slept better the night before. The fear had left me; I had conviction on my side. It was a perfect day, one I will remember always.

Conviction helps us to find enough certainty in order to act. Founders need to present their business case with conviction if they want investors to say "yes." Salespeople need to present their product's value with conviction if they want to get the sale. And team members must show enough conviction to get managers to agree to their plans. You may have data to back up your argument, but there are few facts about the future—that's why conviction is so precious.

"Despite having no experience in fashion, retail, or business leadership, Sara Blakely founded the now well-known shapewear company

Spanx in 2000." She discovered the idea while "attempting to look her best in a pair of white trousers."[2] In essence, she was a frustrated consumer. The men who ran established hosiery firms didn't know or didn't care about the problem that she and millions of women faced. She discovered that they didn't even test their products on real people but used mannequins instead.

Sara "started Spanx with a $0 marketing and advertising budget. The company relied entirely on networking, social connections, and customers' word-of-mouth. . . . Blakely paid her friends to show up in various cities and create hype around her product. When she'd schedule a live demonstration in a store, she'd even pay people to show up and act excited."[3] She made and sold the first version of her legendary leggings herself, even as she worked a day job. Today, her brand is worth more than one billion dollars. Her conviction inspired everyone around her and propelled her company to success.

Conviction, a firmly held belief, can be ignited by passion. According to research by Harvard Business School professor Laura Huang, published in her book *Edge: Turning Adversity into Advantage*, passion is one of the most important qualities of a successful VC startup pitch.[4] Founders rated high on passion were 7.4 times more likely to receive funding than less passionate founders. Product performance, market size, bad data—none of these were as critical as passion.

There can be a dark side to conviction. We have seen the dangers of an overly charismatic founder, which is why we tell horror stories about them: Elizabeth Holmes and Theranos, Billy McFarland and Fyre Festival, Adam Neuman and WeWork. They remind us that conviction without humility and values can be dangerous. But it also highlights the alchemy that conviction provides, especially for less privileged founders. It's elevating. It's magic, so make sure it does good things. More Gryffindor than Slytherin, if you follow Harry Potter.

Reflections on Finding Conviction

1. Do you have conviction about your venture? Where do you have it? Where is it missing and why?

2. If it's missing, what will it take to find your conviction?

3. How does your conviction, or lack of it, really show?

4. Who can help you to find the conviction to power your organization forward?

CHAPTER 29

Making Decisions

We need to accept that we won't always make the right decisions, that we'll screw up royally sometimes—understanding that failure is not the opposite of success, it's part of success.

—Arianna Huffington, May 19, 2019, Twitter post

You are running out of capital. The fundraising environment is increasingly unfriendly to your type of business. Your existing investors are reluctant to commit more. You are trying to protect the longer-term prospects of your business and retain a talented and committed team. But your options are few, and the clock is ticking; you have about two months of runway left. A major operator and partner offers to acquire you for much less than the business is worth, but this would allow you to live to fight another day and protects some jobs. Can you find another solution fast? Less than a year ago, the world was your oyster. Welcome to the life of a founder in tougher times. What should you do?

We never have all the information we need to make the best decision, partly because there are no facts about the future. The other reason is that all of us have biases. How our brains are wired impacts our choices—so each of us, presented with the same facts, might reach different conclusions.

Despite these glitches, there are some things we can do to improve our decision-making when it comes to the big decisions. The small stuff should not occupy us here.

In his book *Principles*, Ray Dalio urges us to "systemize our decision-making."[1] By this, Dalio means we should develop our own principles for decision-making, and his book is rich in principles for life, work, economics, and investment. But for me, his core message is to involve the right people in each significant decision. Do not trust either top-down decisions made by an autocratic leader or democratic decisions made by a majority. Instead, Dalio argues we should weigh heavily the opinions of more capable decision makers—he calls this their "believability weighting." And believability is made up of people who have

> Repeatedly and successfully accomplished the thing in question

> Demonstrated they can logically explain the cause-and-effect relationships behind those conclusions[2]

This kind of approach requires us to expose ourselves to the views of other people who may make us question our judgment. And we need to be OK with that. As a coach, I tend to meet founders who *are* OK with being challenged, but I still come across those who aren't. They can't abandon the ideas they have become too invested in and may be heading for difficulties. We all, without exception, have to learn to be more vulnerable and prepared to be wrong. That's why not being alone and building diverse relationships, the subject of two other chapters (chapters 2 and 4) in this book, are so important. It's OK to be wrong—or at the very least, we don't need to worry as much about being wrong.

So, how should we approach significant decisions?

According to Jeff Bezos of Amazon, there are two basic kinds of decisions you can make:[3]

Type 1: Almost impossible to reverse. Bezos calls them "one-way doors." Think about selling your company or figuratively jumping off a cliff.

Once you make a Type 1 decision, there's no going back. These decisions must be made methodically, carefully, slowly, with great deliberation and consultation.

Type 2: Easy to reverse. Bezos calls these decisions "two-way doors." This might be offering a new service or introducing new pricing. While Type 2 decisions might feel momentous, with a little time and effort (often a lot less than you think), they can be reversed. These decisions can and should be made quickly by high judgment individuals or small groups.

According to Bezos, "As organizations get larger, there seems to be a tendency to use the heavyweight Type 1 decision-making process on most decisions, including many Type 2 decisions. The end result of this is slowness, unthoughtful risk aversion, failure to experiment sufficiently, and consequently diminished invention."[4]

So, if you are facing a big decision, consider some of the ways you can reduce the risk of getting it wrong:

> Know who to involve. Who will bring "believability rating" into the discussion?

> Ensure the process is well-informed, with all relevant data available.

> Be present and create an open space for exchange and discussion, and make sure people feel able to speak out.

> Make sure those who are accountable for the outcomes of the decision have a voice in the decision.

> Be clear about what success looks like and allow that to drive the range of options and evaluate the consequences of each option.

> Consider the purpose and values of the business—let these guide your decision.

> When the decision is made, make it clear to every stakeholder, explain the "why," and put the necessary resources behind it to achieve success.

We must make sure that our people are not afraid to speak out. When NASA's *Challenger* space shuttle broke apart seventy-three seconds into its flight in 1986, all seven crew members died. The cause? A failure of the primary and secondary redundant O-ring seals in a joint in the shuttle's right solid rocket booster; it was caused by record-low temperatures at the launch site, which stiffened the rubber O-rings, reducing their ability to seal the joints. Subsequent investigation has shown that the problems with the O-rings *were known before launch.* Our fears and egos sometimes get in the way of the truth, with potentially catastrophic consequences.

Decisions require courage, especially one-way doors. You cannot guarantee success, but you can reduce your risk of failure.

And if the decision is a "two-way door," don't sweat it. Don't impede progress with your process or procrastination. Exploit the benefits of being nimble. Experiment and course-correct with confidence.

Reflections on Making Decisions

1. Are you ready to face the big decisions any founder must face? Are you ready to fail, not just succeed? Remember, not deciding *is* a decision.

2. Are you mindful of your biases and ready to surround yourself with people with a high "believability rating"?

3. Do you make sure you are surrounded by capable people who feel safe to speak up and disagree with you?

4. Do you weigh which decisions justify a high-quality decision-making process and which demand speed?

5. Are you ready to explain your decisions and fully commit to their execution?

Demonstrating Empathy

Leaders with empathy do more than sympathize with people around them: they use their knowledge to improve their companies in subtle, but important ways.

—Daniel Goleman

A major part of the difference between outstanding and average leaders is linked to emotional intelligence (EI). Research shows that EI is twice as important as IQ and technical expertise combined. And unlike IQ, EI can be learned and improved at any age. Psychologist and *Emotional Intelligence* author Daniel Goleman said, "CEOs are hired for their intellect and business expertise—and fired for a lack of emotional intelligence."[1] A *lack* of empathy is a primary cause of interpersonal difficulties that lead to poor performance and problems with board, employee, and customer relationships.

A study by Catalyst, a global nonprofit, "surveyed nearly nine hundred US employees working across industries to understand the effects of empathetic leadership on their experiences at work." To be clear, an empathetic leader, by their definition, "is a leader who demonstrates care, concern, and understanding for employees' life circumstances." They found that empathy has some significant positive effects. For example, when people reported that their leaders were empathetic, they were more likely to report that they were able to be innovative—61 percent of employees compared to only 13 percent of employees with less empathetic leaders. The same with engagement—76 percent of people who experienced empathy from their leaders reported they were engaged compared with only 32 percent who experienced less empathy. Empathy also boosted retention, inclusivity, cooperation, work-life balance, and mental health.[2]

In an April 2015 article on LinkedIn titled "How Emotionally Intelligent Are You?" Daniel Goleman describes social awareness as referring to "how people handle relationships and awareness of others' feelings, needs, and concerns." As he says, "The Social Awareness cluster contains three competencies:

> "Empathy: Sensing others' feelings and perspectives and taking an active interest in their concerns.

> Organizational Awareness: Reading a group's emotional currents and power relationships.

> Service Orientation: Anticipating, recognizing, and meeting customers' needs."[3]

Goleman believes empathy represents the foundation skill for all the social competencies important for work.

How does empathy work in practice? My wife, Jane, worked in an international law firm for her first job and was assigned to support a major office move. She was to be a key link between the managing partner at the firm and the external contractor. The founder CEO of that contractor's company took the lead on this major project. Jane felt anxious at their first meeting, and he could sense that. He asked her what experience she had, and the answer didn't surprise him: absolutely none, but a readiness to work hard and be helpful. What he said put her at ease immediately. He told Jane, "I'll guide you. Any successes you have are yours; any mistakes are mine. You will do just fine." Her fear was heard, and he created a safe space for her to work and learn. She loved working on that project, and because she felt trusted and able to fail, she was desperate not to let him down. The project was hugely successful.

So, if empathy is valuable, what if you are not naturally empathetic? Let's face it, we all know people who are naturally *very* empathic and others who are, well, a bit more, shall we say, insensitive. There is evidence that empathy can develop very early in life. For example, in a study by Lund University, children as young as two demonstrated an appreciation that others hold different perspectives than their own—with the support of an engaged adult. But even if you don't have that kind of natural ability, it is possible to cultivate and develop empathy. And nothing is more powerful than developing empathy skills during everyday conversations on the job.

Developing empathy starts with self-awareness (see chapter 5) because understanding your own emotions is essential to understanding those of others. Empathy skills involve paying attention to other people—listening, attending to the needs and wants of others, and building relationships. Unless you listen and attend to the other person, you simply cannot empathize with them. It completely lacks credibility. "I know how you feel" doesn't make sense when you've never asked how they feel or really heard the answer. Empathy really kicks in when we ask ourselves, "What is this person really saying here?" Or rather, "What is not being said and maybe needs to be addressed?"

Too many "intelligent" leaders are walking around blindly, using only their powers of reasoning and wondering why everyone doesn't see things their way. Those who lack empathy have a tendency to misread others. They don't ask questions to clarify. They don't pay attention to nonverbal cues. Those people who are analytical by nature will listen to the words, facts, and figures and completely miss the real message of what is being said. In fact, when you consider that only 7 percent of the message is carried in the words and the rest is in the nonverbal cues, then only listening to the content of what is being said may actually be misleading.

Of course, being empathetic is not your sole concern as a leader. You want to achieve your purpose and achieve results. Think of this as seeking an effective balance of focus on the business goals and empathic listening. Here are some useful ways to work on the skills of empathy through practice:

> Have regular 1:1s with team members that intentionally and genuinely balance focus and empathy.

> Develop a list of questions to ask at your next 1:1 with that person. Try to make the questions open-ended.

> Practice listening without interrupting. Wait until the other person has shared their point of view before offering yours.

> Avoid being defensive in order to create an open dialogue where possibilities can be explored freely.

> Allow creative time for others to express opinions and ideas without judgment.

> Practice active listening; always check out the meaning of what was said with the person speaking. Paraphrasing what was said helps to clear up misconceptions and deepen understanding.

Empathy is at the heart of emotional intelligence, which is hugely important for leaders. So, hire leaders strong in emotional intelligence, and hopefully you won't have to fire them!

Reflections on Demonstrating Empathy

1. Are you striking the right balance between a focus on what the business needs and empathy?

2. Do you take the time to really understand what your employees, partners, clients, and others are thinking and feeling?

3. Have you developed a strong platform of self-awareness to enable you to understand the feelings of others?

4. Are you committed to practicing empathy in regular 1:1 meetings?

CHAPTER 31

Motivating People

Far and away, the best prize that life has to offer is the chance to work hard at work worth doing.

—Theodore Roosevelt

Money is not the answer to greater motivation. Behavioral research reveals that monetary rewards or incentives produce only temporary compliance. Of course, money is necessary so people can pay their bills and provide for their families—but once these fundamental needs are met, the psychological benefits of additional money are debatable. I remember introducing a profit share for my Value Partnership team that made a big impact in the year it was introduced. From the second year onward, it became just a calculation—business as usual.

There is little correlation between pay and job satisfaction levels across cultures and geographies. Janine Kruger and Chantal Rootman's 2010 research into small businesses in South Africa looked at seven elements of employee motivation. The study showed that while financial rewards can motivate employees, other significant elements that persuade people to work productively include job interest and meaningful work, recognition and feedback, workplace justice and fairness, strong leadership, working conditions, and milestone rewards. The strongest positive motivator was job interest. The weakest motivator was financial reward.[1]

What's going on here? The truth is that our traditional praise-and-reward strategies for motivating performance are not as effective as our behavior would lead us to believe. A quote from a typical employee shared in *Great Advice* by David Wee sums it up well: "If you don't pay me what I am worth, I will leave. But I will not stay only for the money."[2] Roosevelt was right when he said that the prize is about working hard at work that is worth doing. *Why* we work determines, in considerable measure, how well we perform. And this is another arena where purpose-led enterprises should have a distinct advantage for us to exploit.

To understand how this works, we need to distinguish between intrinsic (direct) motives and extrinsic (indirect) ones. Intrinsic motivators include things like purpose, belonging, and learning. Extrinsic motivators are things like money, recognition, and competition. All these things are interactive rather than additive. In other words, they can undermine or reinforce one another. Even doing the most purposeful work imaginable, employees may still quit if the rewards are marginal. Likewise, employees may quit if the rewards are fabulous but the work is without merit. Alfie Kohn, in his book *Punished by Rewards*, puts it this way: "If rewards do not work, what does? I recommend that employers pay workers well and fairly and then do everything possible to help them forget about money. A preoccupation with money distracts everyone—employers and employees—from the issues that really matter."[3]

So, what really matters? In their book *Primed to Perform*, Lindsay McGregor and Neel Doshi offer data and evidence to make a case for the three essential "direct motivators" every company should use to build long-term success:

> Play—when work stimulates and sparks creativity

> Purpose—attaches meaning and mission to work

> Potential—work that provides a path to personal growth[4]

The authors also identify three "indirect motivators" that result in diminished performance. These include emotional pressure, economic pressure, and inertia. For example, emotional pressure causes people to do things for the wrong reasons. An employee might stay in a job because it confers status, but people motivated by emotional pressure do things they don't really want to do, and they don't do them very well.

Recently, I was talking to Ben, a man in his twenties who was head-hunted for a top advertising agency with a great package. He should have been highly motivated, right? Wrong. In his private life, he makes purpose- and values-driven choices, such as valuing the environment and preferring local, seasonal food over supermarkets. The agency recruited him and—without any culture-building induction or get-to-know-you—immediately put the young man on the account of a major UK supermarket, doing work he could do in his sleep. Despite the status of his current firm, or the easy work, he started to look for a new role within weeks, this time focusing on more strategic work for an agency working specifically with B Corps. The lack of play, purpose, and potential compelled him to look elsewhere.

Think about your motives. More than half of entrepreneurs start a company to be their own boss or build something successfully from the ground up. You know that if the money comes your way, it will likely keep coming, and that if you don't love what you are doing (what McGregor and Doshi call "play"), you probably wouldn't keep going, because building a successful business is *hard*.

If you want to improve employee motivation and engagement, the answer lies in truly dedicating the time to understand what employees really value, individually and collectively. You will do well to understand how to use direct motivators and avoid indirect motivators when influencing and managing.

Identify the direct and indirect motivators for your own role, and then with your team members:

> Play: What aspect of your role do you enjoy most? What would you like to do more of/less of?

> Purpose: What impact are you trying to have? What do you want your legacy to be?

> Potential: Where are you trying to get to? What skills are you working on?

> Inertia: What's blocking you and what could you do? How would you like your role to evolve?

The answers to these questions will shed light on the secret to improving both your motivation and that of your colleagues.

Your actions as a leader are critical for employee motivation and retention. Foster connections, listen, show empathy, encourage people to talk to you, and do what you can to be helpful. Talk about the purpose and values of the business and how each team member makes a difference to the lives and work of your key stakeholders. Encourage greater autonomy and accountability.

The Leadership Compass elements (see chapter 16) will help you to create an environment in which people are motivated. As a leader, you can put purpose at the heart of your work, demonstrate strong values, and design your organization around teamwork and empowerment. These factors create an environment where your culture drives high levels of *collective* motivation.

If you want to boost play, purpose, and potential, consider the following:

> *Play*—redesign roles, encourage experimentation

> *Purpose*—connect work to company purpose, increase customer contact

> *Potential*—aim at developing skills through practice, provide coaching

Don't spend inordinate amounts of time designing complicated, ineffectual reward schemes that make performance contingent upon expensive incentives. Motivation comes from within.

Reflections on Motivating People

1. How well do the work environment and culture you've created help your team find its intrinsic motivation?

2. Specifically, how do you rate the level of play, purpose, and potential you see in your team?

3. Are you dedicating the time to understand what individual team members value and what would enhance their motivation?

4. What will you do to raise the levels of play, purpose, and potential in your team?

CHAPTER 32

Building Trust

The best way to find out if you can trust somebody is to trust them.

—Ernest Hemingway

Teams are often where destructive interpersonal conflict plays out, with serious consequences for the business. I was once asked to coach an underperforming team to become a stronger team, capable of solving some of the significant challenges they faced to get their product released and performing. Here are some of things that individual team members told me in confidence:

> It's confrontational, "elbows out" behavior.

> It feels like a struggle; we are dissolving into silos.

> It can feel like a "knife fight," with blame just under the surface.

> People complain about one another outside the room.

> The team dynamic feels "unsafe."

> We do not speak with one voice.

> We show little vulnerability and high defensiveness.

> We are "saturated" with meetings and multiple opinions.

> We have made the product different but not better multiple times.

This high-risk, multimillion-pound project was already late, over-budget, and not delivering the customer experience—despite the fact that the people on this team were highly talented individuals who believed in the idea of the product they were building. A team is a group of people who trust one another—this team was a team in name only.

Why was trust lacking? In the case of this team, I observed the following issues:

> There was no settled vision or plan—the project felt uncertain even at a late stage.

> The structure didn't enable free-flowing collaboration—roles and decision ownership were "murky," as one person described it.

> The leader was reluctant to close out issues for fear of losing collective ownership, so many items were unresolved.

> The team was assembled—but not built.

Trust doesn't flourish in such "murky" work environments. We need to create the conditions for trust. So, how do you build trust when it is lacking? In the case of this team, I coached them on the following strategies:

> Exploring the feedback and confronting the problems facing them

> Developing a shared plan to solve for the vision, project plan, structure, and governance issues

> Learning more about one another, improving their dialogue, and streamlining decision-making

I also coached the leader on his leadership style, encouraging him to listen better, not tolerate poor behavior, and be more decisive when required to keep the team moving forward.

So, what are the elements of trust? The authors of the book *The Trusted Advisor* developed the trust equation:[1]

$$\text{TRUST} = \frac{\text{Credibility x Reliability x Intimacy}}{\text{Perception of Self-Interest}}$$

Let's break this down. Credibility means having expertise in your field of practice, tapping into the latest thinking, and balancing the proven with the novel. Reliability means prioritizing, choosing commitments wisely, and delivering on your promises. These two factors are perhaps self-evident. But what about intimacy—what does that mean? Ask yourself the following:

> Do people around you feel safe talking about difficult or sensitive agendas?

> Are you a "port in the storm" for your team members who are struggling with difficult objectives or are you constantly adding to the pressure?

> Do you find yourself surprised by bad news or are you kept informed along the way?

I don't think any of the members of the team I have described could honestly respond positively to any of these questions.

The final part of the equation is the most powerful; it is the denominator and, as such, divides all the other parts of the equation. The expressions *I want*, *I need*, and *I think* dominated conversations. Team members so focused on their own needs that they didn't know—or care—what their colleagues felt were the most important agenda items. The project was struggling, and the team was focused on protecting their own interests, careers, and reputations.

We talk about how to build great teams in chapter 38, but let's flag here that trust is the foundation for the challenging conversations that lead to a collective commitment to the team purpose. Intimacy is a starting point for building trust between team members. We need to open up about who we are—share details of our personal lives, share our thoughts, and confide in others about our feelings and doubts. We need to get to know our colleagues personally, understand what their values are, and appreciate what they bring to the table. There is a reason we generally do not trust a stranger and prefer to do business with people to whom we have been personally introduced or are already in our network.

Let's remember that trust is *highly* subjective—and contextual, too. For example, I might trust you to put together my flat-pack furniture but not service my car. During Amazon's first year, 1995, Jeff Bezos tried to raise money by predicting $74 million in sales by 2000. He managed to gather $1 million in seed funding from angel investors. At the time, Amazon.com was a platform for selling books, and Bezos was working out of a garage with a potbelly stove. Amazon went public in May 1997 and delivered $1.64 billion in sales in 1999 alone. The money poured in.[2]

Trust is built on the back of your ability to deliver, or over-deliver, on promises. People are taking a risk on you, and your venture needs to build a reputation for delivering on promises—earnings promises to investors, product/service promises to customers, and employee experience promises to your team. Investors, customers, and employees want to feel safe with you. If you try to deceive them and then let them down, you are not trustworthy. That reputation is yours to live with.

Reflections on Building Trust

1. How trustworthy are you? Do you have a reputation for delivering on promises to your key stakeholders? How could you become more trustworthy?

2. What are trust levels like in your organization? Have you cultivated a work environment where people know what is expected and have what they need to be able to deliver?

3. Are you making smart decisions about whom to trust? Taking the time to make sure that you hire the right people, find the right investors, and build a trustworthy product and relationship with customers?

CHAPTER 33

Having Honest Conversations

Honesty saves everyone's time.

—Marcus Aurelius

When I start a coaching relationship with someone, I am looking for some things in my client. Chief among them is honesty. The moment they say, "I don't know what to do," for example, or "I feel like a fraud." Or any other statement that basically reveals their truth. Then I know we are going to do some valuable work together. And my coachee has effectively told me that they trust me not to exploit that moment of vulnerability.

The same applies to teams. If we can't reveal our true selves, trust will not be present. And we won't speak our truth. We will experience what Patrick Lencioni, in his brilliant book *The Five Dysfunctions of a Team*, tagged "artificial harmony," a kind of phony truce.[1] Or we might experience the opposite: mean-spirited, destructive conflict, which leads to withdrawal in many cases. It all represents a huge waste of time and opportunity. Conflict, of the constructive kind, is *necessary* and *required*. It represents the passionate pursuit of the best possible answer. That's what we want for our businesses, and nothing less will do. Without people weighing in on the discussion, however challenging, our decision won't capture the commitment of the team.

Oppressing the truth is nothing new. On April 12, 1633, the chief inquisitor appointed by Pope Urban VIII began the inquisition of physicist and astronomer Galileo Galilei. Galileo was put on trial for holding the belief that the Earth revolves around the sun, which was deemed heretical by the Catholic Church. He was found guilty, agreed not to teach the heresy anymore, and spent the rest of his life under house arrest. It took more than three hundred years for the Church to admit that Galileo was right and to clear his name of heresy.

Speaking truth to power remains difficult to this day. In my first corporate job, I put together proposals for investment in the development of the leadership group. I had heard that executive team meetings, where I would pitch my proposal, are generally straightforward affairs. However, my proposal for investment was brutally rejected. I later learned that the executive team was simply polite with each other (artificial harmony in action) and that if you wanted anything approved, you needed pre-agreement from the key players. I was new, they didn't trust my proposal, and I hadn't understood how to handle the group. When I spoke to them privately, I won their support.

Learning how to navigate a dysfunctional organization is useful. But honesty is better. And for that we need a healthy culture in which people feel able to speak out. We need to get the difficult issues on the table, confront a strategy that is failing, and have tough conversations about performance. Sooner or later, the truth will come out, and the longer it takes, the more expensive and damaging it is likely to be.

One company had several blind spots:

> Overestimation of importance of technology and product

> Underestimation of importance of marketing and management

> Weak leadership skills and low trust culture

> Slow progress developing mobile app versus retail and online

> No effective governance

> No clear vision or strategy

> Didn't learn from mistakes

Every company has blind spots. Great companies identify them, confront them, and tackle them. The rest repeat the patterns until they learn—or run out of road. The founder shareholders of this company wisely decided to appoint their first professional CEO to take their business forward. But two of them continued to involve themselves in day-to-day operations. They didn't agree with the new CEO's diagnosis of the problems, and this led to battles over key decisions. The lack of effective governance made these problems particularly difficult to resolve.

A lack of honesty can have catastrophic consequences. The collapse of Lehman Brothers is attributed to their exposure to the housing market and subprime loans. Lehman Brothers was deeply invested in mortgage-backed securities (MBSs) by the time the mid-2000s rolled around. In 2003, the company acquired a number of lenders, several of whom focused on providing subprime loans. Huge investments in MBSs, many of which were loaded with subprime mortgage loans, is what triggered the demise of Lehman Brothers.

But underneath this truth was a deeper truth. The leadership of Lehman Brothers "embodied and encouraged a culture that embraced more and more risk. At the same time . . . they created an environment where employees were encouraged to go along to get along."[2] There was a gulf between the senior leaders, especially CEO Dick Fuld, and experienced bankers lower down the hierarchy. Fuld was later described by one insider as "seriously out of touch with reality." He and his senior colleagues pursued growth at all costs. Clients were of secondary importance; they were merely the means by which these goals were achieved.

In his book *Good to Great*, Jim Collins says leadership embraces creating a climate where the truth is heard and brutal facts confronted. "There's a huge difference between the opportunity to 'have your say' and the opportunity to be heard. The good-to-great leaders understood this distinction, creating a culture wherein people had a tremendous opportunity to be heard and, ultimately, for the truth to be heard."[3]

Those in leadership positions must ensure a safe environment, one in which individuals can challenge poor decisions and practices without fear of losing their jobs. Serious discussions are too often avoided, while they actually contribute to a well-functioning team and a healthy culture. Teams that tackle conflicts have vivid and active meetings and look for solutions to the real problem.

The most difficult conversations are where opinions differ, the stakes are high, and emotions are strong. We veer away from such conversations for many reasons. Perhaps we fear upsetting someone or negatively impacting our working relationship with them. Perhaps we are unsure how to make our point or where to start. Maybe we've had a previous bad experience of having a tough conversation with this particular individual. Sometimes it seems easier and quicker to work around the problem. But a conflict that goes unresolved will only fester and cause communication breakdowns to develop. Cooperation and teamwork will lessen, and animosity will build. Results suffer when the sense of togetherness is gone. Conflict avoidance ultimately leads to the departure of your best people.

As startup leaders, we need to strive for a close connection with employees across our company. It requires us to be honest and authentic, *especially* when it comes to sharing bad news or addressing difficult topics. We should focus on what we're hearing, not only what we're saying. We can respect the other person's point of view and should expect them to respect ours. Showing empathy is not an endorsement. Displaying empathy to someone who we might find challenging gives both parties the chance to see the other side of the argument—and this can build bridges.

Lastly, given what I've said, don't put off difficult conversations. After the mental gymnastics of endlessly practicing conversations in your head, actually engaging in a two-way conversation can be inspiring, respectful, and productive.

Now for an honest conversation with yourself.

Reflections on Having Honest Conversations

1. Are people able to speak up safely in my business? How can I be sure about this?

2. Do we put the most important and difficult issues on the agenda for discussion?

3. Do we balance voicing and inquiry as a team? Do we listen and argue our position?

4. Do we allow informed constructive conflict to guide the best decision for the business as a whole?

5. Am I leading my organization honestly? Do I tolerate dishonesty in others?

CHAPTER 34

Hiring Well

In most cases being a good boss means hiring talented people and then getting out of their way.

—Tina Fey, comedian, writer, and actress

The decision to bring in talent arises as the business becomes established and the need to bring in specialists in critical areas becomes clear. Maybe the business needs its first CFO or someone to lead sales in a critical market. Some founder CEOs balk at this—they are used to doing things themselves. Talent does not come cheap, and it brings risk. But you need to inspire and attract talent to take the business to the next level or you will potentially suffocate a great idea.

Recruiting the right talent can give your business a huge boost. Delaying or getting it wrong, particularly in a critical role, might even lead to business failure. So, invest in a quality hiring process, because although it may cost you time, getting it wrong could cost you a whole lot more.

Hiring is hard. Experienced managers know this; founder CEOs find out soon enough. It is inherently uncertain, expensive, and time-consuming, with both parties trying to establish the right fit. What we need to look for is a set of hiring practices that really help to predict performance, avoid excessive risk, and are an efficient use of everybody's time.

Hiring starts with being clear what you are hiring for—in other words, understanding the current and future requirements of the job. Zero in on the critical capabilities that will make or break performance—the two or three capabilities that are tightly interwoven and required for the new hire to succeed. This is what makes the decision turn toward one candidate over another. Ram Charan, writing about this in 2016, calls this "the pivot."[1] We also need to accept that every candidate will have weaknesses—so let's be clear that they can both match the demands of the pivot and that you can accept their weaknesses.

If, for example, you are hiring your first CFO to sort out commercial contracts, get a grip on cash flow management, and add value to business decision-making, it may not be important that they have limited M&A experience or are not deeply strategic. As the business evolves, those requirements (the nature of the pivot) could look very different.

When we look at what we need from any candidate, we should consider multiple dimensions:

> Experience (e.g., industry background)

> Skills (e.g., strategic planning)

> Person (e.g., Play Maker)

> Values (e.g., cultural fit)

> Team (e.g., team impact)

Making these things explicit deals with a classic risk: Some founders are inclined, without realizing it, to recruit in their own image. That makes communication easy, but what you really want is someone who is capable of challenging you, not just supporting you. You're looking for someone you can trust to make decisions and give you the time and space to do what you do best.

Once you have defined what you need and what kind of person you want, you should consider thoughtfully which methods to use, not just chat with people, believing you have magical powers to spot top talent. Generally speaking, the best assessment method is an *assessment center*—a combination of different tasks and activities. The following individual approaches are the most accurate, in descending order:

> Work sample tests or observed performance (e.g., demonstrating relevant job capabilities)

> Ability tests (e.g., critical thinking)

> Personality or behavioral tests (e.g., The GC Index®)

> Interviews (more structured equals better)

Combining methods works best. Interviews are important, even if somewhat unreliable, because they create a dialogue setting that is vital for the candidate, as well as the organization. Research backs up my experience; a single interview is unreliable, however good the interviewer.

Todd Carlisle, an organizational psychologist, and Google's People Analytics Team analyzed Google's hiring process in 2006. They tested exactly how many interviews were necessary to be confident about a new hire (Google was doing up to twenty-five interviews for each candidate at that time). The right number of interviews per candidate, he discovered, was four. This new policy, which Google calls the Rule of Four, dramatically reduced the cost and time to hire.[2]

But Carlisle's research revealed something deeper about the hiring process that has resonance for every business: No one manager at Google was very good alone at predicting who would make a good worker. Four meticulously orchestrated Google interviews could identify successful hires with

86 percent confidence, and nobody at the company—no matter how long they had been there or how many candidates they had interviewed—could do any better than the aggregated wisdom of four interviewers.

There are several reasons to aggregate interview assessments. First, everybody is a little bit biased in one direction or another, and combining assessments mitigates that inevitable bias. Second, sometimes people just have bad interviews, and it's unreasonable to base an entire hiring decision exclusively on one interview performance. Finally, Google's finding suggests there are no "brilliant" hirers in the world. Hiring is hard, and nobody is very good at doing it alone.

A word about onboarding. If you fail to deliver on the promises made during hiring, this failure gets in the way of the establishment of an emotional bond between the new hire and the company. Gallup data shows that only 12 percent of employees strongly agree that their organization does a great job onboarding new employees.[3] Employee turnover can be very high in the first eighteen months of employment. This is expensive and wasteful when you consider the effort that went into hiring and the business impact. Take onboarding as seriously as you do hiring.

Reflections on Hiring Well

1. When you hire, are you clear about what "good performance" means in the role you're recruiting for?

2. Do you identify the essential qualities that will be pivotal in delivering that performance? Do you consider carefully what experience, skills, person, values, and team impact you want to see in the candidate(s)?

3. Do you identify how you are going to objectively assess those factors? Do you use multiple tools or a single tool?

4. Do you involve colleagues thoughtfully? Do you utilize groups instead of individuals to reach your conclusions?

5. Do you allow candidates to shine? How can you give them the opportunity to show their best qualities and to ask their questions?

CHAPTER 35

Letting Go

Never tell people how to do things. Tell them what to do, and they will surprise you with their ingenuity.

—General George S. Patton

The worst boss I ever had insisted on telling me how to do things—frequently after I had just told him what I intended. As a young man, I was left burning with frustration, especially when I felt that I *knew* what I should do and how. Fortunately for everyone, I have been my own boss for more than thirty years. Nevertheless, research shows that I'm not the only one to have strong negative emotional and physiological reactions to unnecessary or unwanted help *and* that it frequently damages interpersonal relationships.

When you are the founder, you create an enterprise rooted in your purpose and values. It's natural for you to have strong feelings about what you want to see and what you don't want to see. That begs a couple of questions:

> - Are you right about what you want?

> - If you are, how do you get more of what you want and less of what you don't want?

Unfortunately, I see too many founders who assume they are right and who over-rely on their authority ("I'm the boss") to get more of what they want. Over time, this will suffocate your firm. Let's explore how that works.

First, you *won't* always get it right. For that reason, to become an effective CEO, you need to be held to account. Founders often do not want to lose any freedom and perceive the idea of a board as time-consuming bureaucracy. One of the reasons it is generally a good idea to establish a board of directors quite early in the life of the business is to establish the principle of good governance and temper your own power as principal shareholder, if that is the case. In some respects, this is another way of showing humility—making yourself accountable to the team, investors, and the board, even when it may not be a legal requirement. Within a couple of years of establishing our business, we created a board to hold me as CEO accountable, provide scrutiny of our actions and performance, and diversify our thinking. A good board should add value and provide insight, not only hold you to account. They should also give you feedback on your performance.

Second, you have to let those talented people that you have (expensively) hired get on with their jobs. There is little point in making such an investment and then acting as if you know best. You have to adjust from doing the work to managing the people who do the work. Lots of managers in mature companies struggle with this adjustment, too. If you cannot adjust, you will not tap into the potential of the people you've hired, and they will leave. The further risk is that you will repeat that mistake. The more you understand *your* strengths, the more you will realize that you should narrow your focus on where you add unquestionable value and let go in other areas. So, if you are a game changer and deep polisher of your company's product, focus your energy in that area and build a team around you with counterbalancing strengths.

Third, you need to work *on* the business, not just work *in* it. The more time you spend bogged down in day-to-day stuff, the more you're working *in* your business and failing to plan for the growth you want. Founders who love their product/service and their customers can get lost in this way unintentionally. Two very talented women co-founders in the travel industry were doing just that until we started coaching. As they struggled to answer my questions about performance or the future, they needed little further encouragement to change. Otherwise, the future of their business was a hostage to fortune.

You begin to realize that as a founder CEO, although in the early stages of your business you feel a lot of agency, over time this becomes diminished. Raising capital is one of the biggest drains on your sense of agency and control as shareholder conditions will need to be met. Employing a talented team is another—as I have already said, there is little point unless you give them some agency and control. There is zero merit in fighting this reality. As you accumulate other stakeholders, never forget that your real power stems from your expertise, your influence, your relationships, and your charisma, not your formal authority. In fact, the more you rely on positional power, the weaker you will seem.

So, how should you manage if micromanagement is such a bad approach? Even talented people doing critical work in areas you are not expert in need more than just superficial advice or encouragement. They need assistance that is both well-timed and appropriate to their challenges. In an article in *Harvard Business Review* called "How to Help (Without Micromanaging)," Colin Fisher, Teresa Amabile, and Julianna Pillemer describe three key strategies for being a boss without micromanaging:

> Time your help so it comes when people are ready for it.

> Clarify that your role is to be a helper.

> Align the rhythm of your involvement—its intensity and frequency—with people's specific needs.[1]

As a coach, I am experienced at timing my help when someone is ready for it. This is because we learn mostly through practice (remember, "clarity comes from engagement and not thought"), and so rather than give some-one a full guide to something, I let them experiment and come back with questions. We all learn through progression, so too much guidance or information before someone understands the need for it is unhelpful. Start where they are rather than where you are.

Managers need to make it clear that when they are getting involved, it is *to help*. Otherwise, the suspicion may be that the team member is failing in some way and the manager does not fully trust them. Great managers create a climate where it is OK to not know and to ask for help. In that climate, when the manager offers to step in to help, the team member learns to trust that intention and value that help.

In one case, a founder was proud of his exceptional ability to build trusted relationships with clients and commercialize these. No one else in the firm could come close. The business was overly dependent on that founder's competence, which severely limited the firm's scalability. That is, until he started to intentionally share his contacts and skills with his team—and upgraded that team over time. Instead of sweeping in to win the client, he learned to step back, coach, and limit his involvement, as well as its intensity and frequency, to the needs of his team.

Avoiding micromanagement does not mean avoiding managing. It means being thoughtful and clear with your team about your intention and the nature and timing of your involvement. Develop your team to be confident, capable, and accountable. The best people will want to come and work for you—I guarantee it.

Reflections on Letting Go

1. How much have you done to make yourself, as founder CEO, accountable?

2. To what extent are you working *on* the business or *in* it? Are you clear about how the business is performing and where it is going?

3. How well are you managing your team to maintain their accountability, foster their growth, and capitalize on their talent?

4. How thoughtful and clear are you with your team about your intentions and the nature and timing of your involvement?

CHAPTER 36

Managing Performance

People on your team want two things: Make me feel a part of something bigger than me and make me feel special.

—Marcus Buckingham, author and speaker

So, how do you get the best out of the people in your team? Some of the things already explored in the book will contribute to that end:

> When you hired them, you were clear about the performance expectations of the role (chapter 34).

> You engaged them in strategy setting so they share your conviction in the company vision and two to three focused objectives (chapter 21).

> You are managing them to be confident, capable, and accountable rather than telling them what to do (chapter 35).

These things will help set you up for success, but what is the best way to secure high performance from each member of your team?

Large corporations have traditionally relied on annual formal and structured conversations that look backward, focus on ratings, and achieve little more than dread from managers and team members alike. People hate performance evaluations. They really do. According to a 2018 survey of Fortune 1000 companies done by the Corporate Executive Board (CEB), 66 percent of employees were strongly dissatisfied with the performance evaluations they received in their organizations.[1] A mountain of data tells us that this approach simply doesn't work, yet 90 percent of the Fortune 500 persist with it. Good news, fellow founder, you can do what you like!

So, let's design a better approach. What do we want? Here are some suggestions for you to consider:

> Foster a growth mindset.

> Provide support or challenge them when needed.

> Inspire and make them feel valued.

> Promote high performance in the near-term future.

Regular meetings are essential to track progress, solve problems, and learn/pivot. This is sometimes referred to as the "cadence of accountability." These 1:1s are your opportunity to "performance manage" your way.

Bestselling author Marcus Buckingham encourages us to see the year as fifty-two short sprints. He suggests checking in every week with each team member for fifteen minutes in order to ensure alignment on focus and expectations. Not once a year—once a week. Or, as Marcus asks, are you too busy to do that? Doing what, out of curiosity? This is leadership work. And here's the core check-in question: "What are your priorities this week and how can I help?"[2] In asking this, we aren't telling people where they stand; we are helping them to *get better*.

Neuroscientists like David Rock have shown us that with the right context and conditions, *anyone's* abilities can be improved, especially given the expansive, flexible nature of the human brain.[3] So, it absolutely makes sense to regularly check in with each team member in a way that encourages them to get better. These are coaching moments, valuable for the individual and informative for you. It will give you confidence (or not) that the business will achieve what it is aiming at.

Because these conversations are frequent and focused on the here and now, they allow for constant adaptation to the unpredictable environment we face, and they avoid difficulties going unspoken or unaddressed for weeks on end. They do not, however, do *everything* we need, given their near-term focus. We need to help people to stand back from near-term performance to reflect. And we can do more to foster that all-important growth mindset (see chapter 1).

One British AI technology firm has introduced the weekly check-in system and, alongside it, asks their managers to have quarterly conversations with their people with a clear focus on *learning* and *engagement*. They have four simple questions for discussion:

> Pride—What has made you proud of your work (this last quarter)?

> Learning—What would you do differently (individual retros/learnings) from the work you did this last quarter?

> Support—What help and support do you need from me to be even more impactful?

> Priorities—What will you be focused on during the next quarter?

These conversations are naturally longer but create the opportunity for a deeper coaching experience and a more strategic focus. Notice also how they connect to those core motivators we discussed earlier in the book—play, purpose, and potential (see chapter 31).

What's the secret to a great conversation like this? And what happens *after* the conversation? After all, we want to improve performance, right?

> Create action items. A necessary part of moving the team member along in their work and growth is to take action. Agree on clear expectations and timelines. Write these down. Make a plan together.

> Take coaching notes. Provide these for your team member to look back on when they encounter similar challenges in the future. Help them improve.

> Take action. Do what you say you'll do. It shows team members that they matter, that their work matters.

> Follow up. One-on-ones only work when they are held regularly and consistently. Keep this commitment, and you'll create a cadence of feedback and a culture of accountability.

So, now we have the building blocks of a performance management process: frequent check-ins and deeper quarterly conversations, all based on a coaching model to foster a growth mindset.

One more thing needs consideration. Whatever system you use to set objectives (e.g., objectives and key results—OKRs), how do you agree on goals at the right level? The human brain loves a challenge, but only if it is within an optimal zone of difficulty. The Goldilocks Rule (which has been applied across multiple disciplines) states that humans experience peak motivation when working on tasks that are right on the edge of their current abilities. Not too hard. Not too easy. Just right. (For those from different cultures, the Goldilocks Rule is named after the fairy tale *Goldilocks and the Three Bears*.)

As psychologist Gilbert Brim put it, "One of the important sources of human happiness is working on tasks at a suitable level of difficulty, neither too hard nor too easy."[4] This blend of happiness and peak performance is sometimes referred to as *flow*, which is what athletes and performers experience when they are "in the zone." Flow is the mental state you experience when you are so focused on the task at hand that the rest of the world fades away.[5] Then you can truly shine. And we want the people in our teams to shine, don't we?

Reflections on Managing Performance

1. Do you have an established approach to performance management that you use? How well is it working?

2. Do you have regular, frequent check-ins with members of your team that enable them to perform better?

3. Are you coaching team members, encouraging a growth mindset, and really helping members of your team to perform better?

4. Are the objectives they are working on set at the right level (the Goldilocks Rule)?

CHAPTER 37

Developing People

Growth is painful. Change is painful. But nothing is as painful as staying stuck somewhere you don't belong.

—Mandy Hale, author

Let's start with a growth mindset and the knowledge that everyone who works for us has the potential for growth. We adopt an approach to leadership that gives space and expects results rather than overmanages people. We offer help when we sense it's needed. If we are doing these things, we are already acting in ways that will foster growth. But there is more we can do.

In this chapter, I want to talk about your role as a coach. Yes, yours, not mine! I also want to explore the barriers to personal development, since sometimes people remain stubbornly stuck. And lastly, I want to explore how we can overcome some of those barriers. Because a significant part of the answer lies with you, their leader.

But first, why is this issue so important? Organizational psychologist Tomas Chamorro-Premuzic suggests that too many leaders achieve their positions by being self-centered, overly confident, narcissistic, arrogant, manipulative, and risk-prone.[1] These behaviors destroy trust and lead employees to look elsewhere to pursue their careers. Research shows that most people find their managers to be far from ideal; for example, in a recent survey, 75 percent of survey participants said that the most stressful aspect of their job was their immediate boss.[2] All of this is very costly. A 2018 workforce activity study by Global Talent Monitor found that 40 percent of employees who left their jobs cited a "lack of future career development" as a primary motivator for quitting.[3]

Feeling a sense of progress and mastery—and hence having well-organized work and the right skills for the job—is key to feeling fulfilled. If you demonstrate a commitment to your team and their personal growth and create an environment in which this growth can develop strong roots, your team will be happier, perform better, and want to go further on your business journey with you. In my experience, many leaders themselves are happier and find their roles more meaningful when they feel they are helping other people. So, given that, what can we do?

Growth does not come without hard work. And sometimes without some pain. When I train to run a marathon, the work is daily and the gains only emerge over time, something known as delayed gratification. The pain is real and physical and immediate. Training through a British winter requires grit. It would be so easy to give up. The same rules apply to the growth of one of your team members. The pain may not be physical, but trying something new will feel uncomfortable at first. And progress will take time and patience.

In my experience, the barriers to growth fall into three categories:

> *Lack of self-insight:* Sometimes people have a rather rigid self-concept ("that's the way I am") or are in denial about their need to grow (to maintain appearances). Or it may be a failure to understand the "why." There are many potential reasons we may fail to grasp opportunities for growth. Often, we are unaware of them.

> *Motivational:* Success sometimes breeds complacency. Others tell us we are fine as we are. We may try to avoid the discomfort of growth. And there is a phenomenon of being criticized for behaving differently and rewarded for staying the same. Our "friends" sometimes hold us back, quite unintentionally.

> *Behavioral:* Insight is not always enough. Motivation is also not enough. We need to know what will work better—not generalized aspirations but concrete actions we can practice. And not waiting for the right moment, because clarity comes from engagement, not thought. A failure to persevere, monitor, and receive ongoing feedback and reinforcement may also hold us back.

These barriers, when we consider them in the round, illustrate why personal development is hard. A lack of external support makes it harder, and that's where you come in. Make sure you are a learning resource and coach, rather than an authoritarian boss obsessed with maintaining a strong image. If you can model some humility and a growth mindset, others may well follow suit. When leaders go first, others will follow.

On a practical level, you can do (at least) three big things to support members of your team:

1. *You can help them to see themselves accurately.* Offer thoughtful feedback that helps them to understand the impact of their actions: "This is what I observe and its impact." Explore with them what factors, triggers, or indicators—both negative and positive—prompt them to behave in certain ways (e.g., getting overly involved in the work of the team). Help them to think about when to utilize a personality trait to their advantage and when it's best to leave it on the side lines (e.g., a desire to help others).

2. *You can help them to find their motivation to grow, to understand the "why."* Why is the behavior you are looking at undermining their performance? Why will they need to master this behavior to

advance their career? For example, a manager who "steps in" to tell their team members what to do will undermine their confidence and not demonstrate readiness for a more senior role. The more you understand what drives your team member, the better you will be able to help them to find their "why."

3. *You can provide coaching to unlock new behaviors and habits.* I believe coaching should be a part of everyone's leadership role. In the last chapter on performance management, we looked at regular 1:1 conversations that create the opportunity for a coaching experience. But how can you structure and approach a coaching conversation?

Perhaps the most common and simplest tool that coaches use is the GROW coaching framework, originally developed by Sir John Whitmore, which is based on the following questions:

> Goal—What do you want to work on? What is your goal for this?

> Reality—What is happening currently? Invite self-assessment. Ask them to provide examples.

> Options—What options do you have? Invite and offer suggestions.

> Will—What specifically will you do, by when? Make commitments.[4]

It sounds simple. From experience, these are my tips:

> Listen well, use more "ask" than "tell"—80 percent of the time the individual should be talking (don't ask endless questions, for example).

> Elicit ideas from the individual—don't try to prove you are smart, and don't think you need to have all the answers.

> Develop ideas together, but only when the issue is understood (don't converge on solutions too quickly).

> Seek to understand, not to judge (be supportive; change is difficult).

> Work on practical behaviors and actions (don't get all psychological).

You won't get it right the first time, and it will never be perfect. But don't let that stop you. Voltaire said, "Perfect is the enemy of good." And as Matthew Syed said, "purposeful practice," with enough quantity, quality, and feedback, is the bedrock of ability.[5] Don't let a few weeks of halfhearted effort at coaching confirm any false beliefs you might have about this. Delayed gratification is real, so let's keep practicing and trust in the outcome.

Reflections on Developing People

1. Are you ready to demonstrate a commitment to your team and their personal growth? Do you trust in the value of this action?

2. Are you creating opportunities to get to know your team members and to give them feedback and coaching?

3. Do you see coaching as a part of your role and are you ready to practice coaching with members of your team?

CHAPTER 38

Building a Great Team

Great things in business are never done by one person. They're done by a team of people.

—Steve Jobs

I t always amazes me how *little* thought and effort many businesses put into building their leadership team. In so many areas of life, we see the exceptional results that can be achieved through carefully assembled teams and practiced teamwork: the pinpoint precision of the Red Arrows aerobatics team, the smooth synchronization and power of an Olympic Eight in rowing. Consider the care that a Premier League coach takes to select players based on their technical ability, their mentality, their ability to switch positions, and their level of conditioning. And then think about the work they do to prepare for and achieve high levels of performance and adaptability under competitive pressure—the trust, discipline, behaviors, and communication required. Yet what do we see in far too many businesses? Teams where trust is absent, that have become battlegrounds where individual needs take precedence over the goals of the team. Teams that have no shared goals or standards of behavior. Teams that have poor meetings when people are barely present while business challenges are discussed.

It makes no sense at all for a business to assemble an expensive team of functional experts and then put little or no effort into creating the conditions for collective high performance. It is noticeable that individuals who are known for their exceptional talents frequently stress the value of teaming. Michael Jordan, the legendary basketball player, put it this way: "Talent wins games, but teamwork and intelligence win championships."[1] It's high time businesses raised their game and applied "teamwork and intelligence" to their work. Let's explore what that would look like. The prize is worth it. There is a 1.9 times increased likelihood of having above-median financial performance when the top team is working together toward a common vision, according to Scott Keller and Mary Meaney in their 2017 book *Leading Organizations: Ten Timeless Truths*.[2]

Most investors think the quality of the management team is vital. But they tend to think of it as the sum total of the experience and skill assembled rather than the extent to which they realize the synergies available to them. Of course, they both matter. Based broadly on a groundbreaking 1993 book by Jon Katzenbach and Douglas Smith called *The Wisdom of Teams*, there are five essential disciplines that I believe we need to work on:

1. *Common purpose and values:* The team must be involved in shaping this for it to be genuinely *common*.

2. *Shared performance goals and strategy:* These are compelling goals that *require* teamwork to achieve.

3. *Mutual accountability:* The process of agreeing on goals serves as the crucible in which members forge their accountability *to one another*.

4. *Complementary skills:* Appropriate diversity including expertise, experience, the mix of personalities, and the different types of impact that team members bring.

5. *Shared commitment to how we work together:* The team agrees who will do what, how decisions will be made, and what behaviors are expected from one another.[3]

When working as a team coach, one of the first things that I do is talk to the CEO and then to individual team members to find out what it is like to be a member of that team. The picture that emerges typically gives a vivid insight into the dynamics of the group. One such team could be summarized with the following characteristics (a real example):

> A strong sense of team now (a big step up from where we were)

> Healthier dialogue as a whole team

> Seeking to clarify our "lanes" (not "turf wars"—intentions are good)

> More regular meetings helping us align better

> Team relationships strengthened through strategic planning effort

> Super-stretched and exhaustion experienced by team members

> Misunderstandings arise—working virtually contributes

> Need for executive team meetings to be more strategic

> Going into great detail makes us overly tactical

> Need for more time to think freely

> Still too much weight of the business on the CEO's shoulders

> Still an unwillingness to tackle difficult issues in the team

Surfacing issues like these and then discussing them openly with the team creates a platform for genuine team problem-solving. According to

McKinsey.com, "Teams need to regularly take stock of and improve their operating rhythm, meeting protocols, interaction quality, and dynamics"—with or without a team coach.[4]

Each of the five essential disciplines listed previously can be worked on. I have talked about common purpose, strategy, and goal setting elsewhere in this book. So, let's look at numbers 4 and 5. As I mentioned earlier, complementary skills are multidimensional. For example, the right diversity of impact can help to design a great team. The GC Index®, introduced in chapter 5, is a powerful enabler of insight and progress for this. Take a look at this leadership team of a fast-growing fashion business in 2019 and then again in 2020 (this business is at stage 4 based on the chapter 15 business journey: "scaling up and professionalizing").

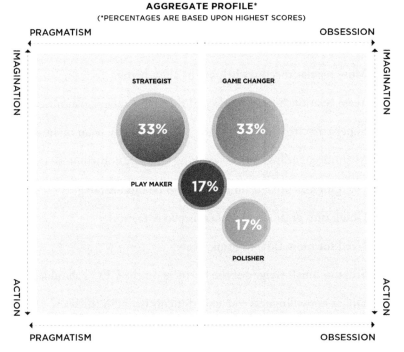

Figure 38.1. Image by permission of The GC Index®. All rights reserved.

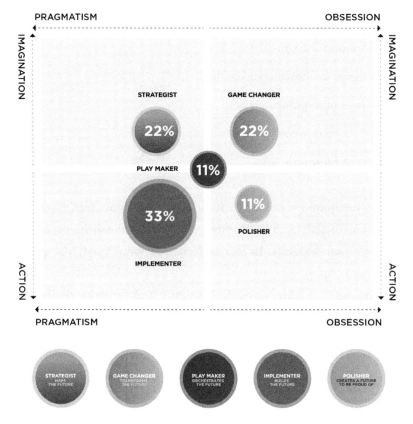

Performance problems emerged in 2019 as the company struggled to consistently execute well—the CEO was becoming over-involved in some parts of the business as a consequence. The team was strengthened in areas such as operations and digital marketing. The appointment of very execution-driven individuals in these roles rebalanced the whole team in 2020, which is now securing growth in a much more sustainable way.

The fifth discipline, a shared commitment to how we work together, requires the team to recognize the reality of their existing dynamics and commit to new ones. Patrick Lencioni gives us an elegant framework for understanding team dynamics in his *Five Dysfunctions of a Team*. I prefer the positive version of the dysfunctions—the five *functions*:

> Demonstrate trust.

> Engage in constructive conflict.

> Commit to group decisions.

> Hold peers accountable.

> Focus on team results.

Each is required in order to achieve the next. Without trust, there will be no constructive conflict. Without conflict, there will be no commitment to group decisions. In that context, you won't hold your peers to account or focus on team results.

Teams need to learn through experience and feedback the behavior they need to enhance to perform better. Do people need to stop having the meeting outside the conference room, backsliding on decisions, or showing disrespect for one another? The top team of a highly successful business cocreated these simple rules for themselves and reviewed them often:

> This is our first team (our own teams are second).

> There are no hidden agendas (get it "on the table").

> Everyone needs to find their voice on all the key issues (no functional silos).

> Challenge one another (to ensure we make the best decision).

> Support one another (especially when the pressure is on).

> Disagreement inside the team is fine; outside it is not (speak respectfully about one another always).

> Be clear at the point of decision (accountable for delivery to one another).

It's also vital to agree on the right meeting cadence to suit the nature of your business and the challenges you face. For example, short weekly check-ins on performance and longer but well-managed monthly meetings on strategic goals.

If you can establish the right disciplines and dynamics in your team, you will yield huge benefits across the business. This will take a load off your CEO shoulders and enable you to look both forward and outward.

Reflections on Building a Great Team

1. Do you have the right composition in your team?

2. What about the five disciplines—how would you rate your team on them today?

3. The same goes for the five functions—establishing healthy team dynamics. How would you rate your team dynamic?

4. What actions will you take to transform your team into a high-performing team?

CHAPTER 39

Understanding Finance

You've got to understand accounting. You've got to. That's got to be like a language to you.

—Warren Buffett, 2020 interview with
Yahoo! Finance's editor in chief, Andy Serwer

worked as a ski instructor in Austria for a season in my mid-twenties. Ever since then, I've always wanted to know where I am on the mountain, the snow conditions, the weather forecast, and the condition and energy levels of the people skiing with me in order to make the best decisions. I trained my daughter to see all of these things when she was growing up, and she went on to become a ski instructor herself. Similarly, being always aware of the financial condition and financial outlook of your business is really important. It is your responsibility as the steward of your business. Do not simply delegate it to others. Learn about it—learn the language of accounting and speak it.

Finance is another area where the Goldilocks Rule applies. *Too much* focus on finance is like looking at the scoreboard when you should be playing the game to win. And if you are purpose-led, the score does not represent your central goal. *Too little* focus on finance, and you risk business failure. A character called Bill in Ernest Hemingway's book *The Sun Also Rises* poses a question: "How did you go bankrupt?" The answer from another character, Mike, was, "Two ways. Gradually, then suddenly."[1] So, whether you are focused on the money or not, it's wise to pay *just the right amount* of attention to it.

In the worst of circumstances, such as when you are running out of money, managing your cash position becomes a life-and-death issue. Some years ago, traditional news media firms became aware that advertising revenues for print were falling off a cliff as big clients moved their resources to online and social media. A trend became a deluge that required a rapid change in the strategy and business model of news media and many other media organizations. Some technology firms have recently had to confront the fact that their future fundraising has become significantly more difficult or expensive. Based on their burn rate (the rate at which they use up capital), they can calculate when their cliff edge will be reached. Reducing that burn rate to a manageable level and making their company profitable has become an urgent priority for cash-burning, higher-risk technology companies.

But there are more reasons for giving your venture's finances the right amount of attention than avoiding catastrophic failure. Here are some important ones:

> *Focus on cash.* Cash is more important than anything else for a young business. Build a strong cash management plan from the outset. Know where you stand on cash on hand. Even if you have a brilliant team, they won't stay if you can't pay them. Manage invoicing well. Don't wait until the end of the month to issue invoices; send them as soon as the work is complete. Michael Dell put it this way: "We were always focused on our profit and

loss statement. But cash flow was not a regularly discussed topic. It was as if we were driving along, watching only the speedometer, when in fact we were running out of gas."[2]

> *When forecasting, look for realism, not optimism.* You might want the business to grow at a certain rate, but the market might have other ideas, or your team might not be capable of delivering. Avoid a false sense of security based on an unrealistic forecast. I've seen the damage done by both investors and CEOs who drive people to forecast results to keep them happy based on a *complete lack of realism.* It's like taking a drug and going cold turkey. It encourages spending that the business can ill afford. It damages the culture and kills businesses.

> *Understand what improves performance.* In other words, know which levers to pull. If you understand what drives margin in your business, you can start to make really smart decisions. For most businesses, there are four major profit drivers: price, variable costs (i.e., those costs that vary in direct proportion to revenue, typically represented by cost of sales), fixed costs (or overhead), and sales volume. Revenue does not pay the bills or give you the resources you need to grow— that comes from profit. An increase in price has the greatest impact because every additional pound goes straight to profit. In my consultancy business, I made it a rule not to negotiate on price. We would be generous with our time but not concede *an inch* on price because it would kill our margin. If you have no consistency on price, not only do you create more work through negotiations, but you also risk losing track of receivables.

> *Understand the impact of your business model.* The choices you make about which customers to serve, which products to offer, and your price/positioning drive your financial results. A travel destination management company (DMC) I worked with was looking

to transform their business into a luxury DMC. We analyzed the attractiveness of existing clients on four criteria:

› Profitability

› True partners (honest, know their clients, discerning)

› Recognize the true value of their services

› Aspirational client in luxury segment

This has evolved into a prequalification tool for clients. By confidently pricing their products or services, dealing only with those customers who see the value they deliver, and not allowing price-sensitive customers or competitors to dictate their company's pricing strategy, the profit is starting to flow.

> *Value your own contribution properly.* For a clear view on the company's profitability and financial health, you need to factor in your salary needs. Even if you can't afford to pay out cash to yourself yet, track it. All too often, founders neglect themselves. The risk of starting a business has to be worth it. You need cash to live on. Don't let the business struggle on as a vanity project you really cannot afford to sustain or that has no exit reward.

> *Growth is expensive.* Plan for it carefully. Growth costs money and places stress on your working capital. It could be for hiring, production costs, other operational overheads, or simply the increase in the cash cycle to fund the increase in debtors pending payment. Don't spend money that you haven't received yet. Hold off on new hires or expansion plans until the cash is actually in the bank. Getting that the wrong way around is painful.

> *Bookkeeping is too important to overlook.* Make sure you have good, reliable financial information available to you, such as a simple software tool like Xero. If you are beyond the startup stage, hire a finance manager who can help to keep track of and manage the financial side

of the business. At the growth and scale-up stages, you need a CFO who can help you think about the more strategic financial and commercial challenges that will arise.

Reflections on Understanding Finance

1. How well do you understand the numbers underpinning your business?

2. How good are your instincts about the financial consequences of the decisions you make?

3. Do you have an honest and realistic view of the future financial trajectory of your enterprise and its funding requirements and how these can be met?

4. How well set up is your business in terms of financial management and information? Do you know where you stand at any moment?

5. What improvements are needed in the financial management of your business?

CHAPTER 40

Managing Investors

Marry in haste, repent at leisure.

—William Congreve, in *The Old Bachelor* (1693)

Twenty years after founding his business, one founder CEO is dissatisfied with his cash earnings and his long-term equity incentive and is in dispute with his board and the private equity interests represented there. Like other founders, he is heavily invested in his business. Over those twenty years, he and his wife remortgaged their first house to start the company, used personal savings to pay salaries and suppliers, and remortgaged the house again to invest in IP and technology when it was needed. He could earn significantly more in the employment market. His value to the business is still absolutely pivotal. All he wants is a base salary solution that will allow him to focus on doing his job and build a great, profitable, and increasingly cash-generative business. Unfortunately, the private equity deal he struck some years ago was with the wrong people. A compromise was reached on his deal in the end, but the wrong people are still around. I want to explore how we can *avoid* this all-too-common problem.

The first investor you need to manage is you. You are investing your time and money in the venture from day one. That has both a real cost and an opportunity cost; for example, what would your salary be if you stayed employed? What is your calculation for investing in this venture—what returns are you basing that investment on, tangible or intangible? This calculation is important at the beginning, and it is still important deep into the journey of the venture, as the previous story illustrates.

At some point in your business journey, you are likely to need someone else's money to grow and scale your business. The basic choice is debt or equity. When CEOs of early-stage companies think about growth capital, they rarely think of debt financing. Maybe it's the interest rate or repayment cap attached. Maybe it's the ubiquity of venture capital. The truth is, if you plan to grow and scale, debt is cheaper than equity, and you stay in control of your business. Lenders don't need to keep up with your every decision, and they don't require board meetings. And also keep in mind that raising a VC round usually takes between six and nine months of meetings, pitches, and phone calls, which can be a huge distraction from running your business. Raising debt financing is generally much faster.

Unfortunately, debt is not always available as an option for founders. There must be sufficient operating cash flow generated by the enterprise to service the debt's interest and principal payment obligations, or there could be severe consequences. Lenders can foreclose, possibly requiring the business to cease operations and liquidate its assets. So, *too much* debt can present an existential risk. It might be that convertible notes (a form of short-term debt that converts into equity) or SAFEs (simple agreement for future equity) to raise pre-seed funds from friends, family, and angels can be helpful as they allow you to get going quickly without having to put a precise value on your company.

Now, let's consider venture capital. In talking with investors and founders, there seem to be a few golden rules:

> Don't raise money unless it's necessary.

> Don't raise money when you are desperate.

> The axiom of "only raise what you need" has evolved to "raise what you need but bake in a bit of a cushion" because of market volatility.

> Seek to assess how much capital you need not just for the current round of funding, but also for the entirety of the journey to the point of exit.[1] Your strategy should define those needs and their timing.

You need to understand the investor mindset. Venture capitalists are contractually bound to be LP (limited partner) friendly first—meaning they have to produce returns. That's what drives the push for different valuations, various types of control, and a host of other behaviors. Founders need to face into that reality. Every time you go through a funding round, you are being diluted. Industry experts estimate that founders will probably sell 20 to 35 percent of their company during their series A round. And VCs know that many of the businesses in their fund will fail to deliver the returns they want. If you are one of those businesses, prepare for them to lose interest in your fate. It isn't personal; it's just the way the VC world works. Peter Thiel, co-founder of PayPal, put it this way: "The biggest secret in venture capital is that the best investment in a successful fund equals or outperforms the entire rest of the fund combined."[2]

However, more and more VCs talk about being *founder friendly*. Let's be clear what that means. It's not the outcome that drives "friendliness"; it's how honestly, consistently, and ethically the investor acts. And it's whether they act in a way that recognizes the real drivers of value creation, such as a talented team. That's why the biggest lesson of all for founder leaders about managing investors is finding the right ones in the first place. They are out there; you just need to find them. So, do your research and take advice.

So, as a purpose-driven founder, what would a great investor look like?

> They share your purpose. This would be a big win.

> They bring operational experience and therefore can add value through mentorship or a board seat. They may also bring a network of powerful connections that can accelerate the growth of the business (e.g., through a joint venture).

> They empathize with the challenges, motivations, and risks the founder has to deal with every day. Ex-founders who have moved into venture capital are naturally more empathetic than the first generation of ex-banker VCs.

> They take into account all the stakeholders in the longer-term interests of the business because they all impact the success of the enterprise.

> Their term sheets are fair and straightforward, not loaded with onerous terms such as *liquidation preferences* and *ratchet clauses.*

> They do not undermine the interests of the business in pursuit of their own. They understand that even if the founder is no longer the majority owner, the founder should not have to face an unsupportive or divided board.

The moment you take significant amounts of money from outside investors, the importance of governance is put in sharp focus. In a 2019 *Forbes* article, Tim Young, a founding general partner at Eniac Ventures, says, "Too often, founders focus on financing at the expense of governance. The wisest founders know to treat board composition with the same priority as deal economics."[3]

What Tim is talking about is maintaining control of your company. Once you lose control of your board, you are unlikely to regain it. There will come a time when letting go becomes the right thing for both the venture and you. But how much better to be in control of both the timing and the process!

A final reality check here. You can't secure VC funding without making certain assurances. When a firm puts thousands or millions of dollars behind your company, it expects a return on this investment. You will need to commit to certain milestones, growth targets, and deliverables, which can add a great deal of pressure. Avoid overpromising to secure an investor and then under-delivering; it only adds to the pressure and damages the essential trust between you and your fellow investors. You may need to call on that trust one day.

Reflections on Managing Investors

1. Since you are the first investor, perhaps along with your partner(s), do you have a clear idea of the returns you're looking for? And are you sensibly protective of those interests?

2. Do you have a strategy and business plan that makes clear what the investment needs of the business are and the timing of those needs?

3. Have you done your homework on the best type of funding for your particular business and situation? Are you clear-sighted about the "rules of the game"?

4. All money is not the same. Do you have a clear idea of what you are looking for from an investor? How will you determine if they are founder friendly?

5. Is your governance and board fit for purpose? Do you have a board that is working well with you as CEO?

6. How is the relationship with existing investors working—are you playing your part? Are they delivering on their promises? What would strengthen the trust between you?

CHAPTER 41

Managing Customers

Strive not to be a success, but rather to be of value.

—Albert Einstein

I had the privilege of observing a Guidance Team lineup in a five-star Ritz-Carlton hotel on the Indian Ocean one morning. (*Guidance Team* is their term for the leadership team of a property.) It is the job of every GM to ensure a lineup is held for every shift, every day, and used as a method for reinforcing the Gold Standards. The motto "We are Ladies and Gentlemen serving Ladies and Gentlemen" is undoubtedly the best-known part of the Gold Standards. It is made clear to every employee that they must treat Ritz-Carlton guests with dignity and act the same way toward their colleagues. The lineup is used partly to talk about how to personalize guests' individual experiences. Voice of the Customer data is discussed daily. Delivering the finest personalized service is the *primary* business strategy of Ritz-Carlton.

In fact, as Catherine Morin writes, to set the foundation for the exemplary level of customer experience Apple stores are recognized for providing, Steve Jobs relied on his own employees' experiences for inspiration. When asked, most employees cited the Ritz-Carlton as having the best customer service. Morin writes, "So, Jobs sent all his future store managers to Ritz-Carlton hospitality training, which emphasizes the brand's philosophy of offering personalized service and anticipating guests' needs. These techniques eventually set the foundation for Apple stores. Walk into an Apple store today and you'll notice the same personable and straightforward approach to customer service as the Ritz-Carlton."[1]

Much is written on the subject of the customer lifecycle and the huge variety of methods available to both win and satisfy customers. This challenge varies between B2B and B2C businesses, of course. Our interest is in the leadership challenges around securing and delivering for customers.

Ritz-Carlton is a mature business with a deeply embedded culture for addressing the needs of customers. What can they teach a startup or a scale-up? Quite a few things actually:

> Customers come to them because they love the brand and product. In many ways they don't need to be sold. Even if you are a small startup, that is something to aspire to.

> They seek to personalize the customer experience; they don't just standardize it.

> There is deep respect for customers at every level of the organization. Culture is at the heart of the customer experience. Customers generate the revenue, but employees drive the experience.

> Rituals are used to reinforce the mindset and behavior desired on a daily basis. Leaders must exemplify those mindsets and behaviors.

> They make customers the priority and fully appreciate the economics of customer satisfaction and retention.

According to PwC, "73 percent of all people point to customer experience as an important factor in their purchasing decisions."[2] The same research shows that if the customer experience is good, you can charge a premium for it, across *all* sectors. That price premium goes straight to the bottom line.

And according to Bain & Company, the creators of NPS (net promotor score), a 5 percent increase in customer retention produces more than a 25 percent increase in profit.[3]

Why? Return customers tend to buy more from a company over time. As they do, your operating costs to serve them decline. What's more, return customers refer others to your company. And they'll often pay a premium to continue to do business with you rather than switch to a competitor with whom they're neither familiar nor comfortable. Dissatisfied customers churn in a heartbeat. Bad customer reviews spread like wildfire and damage your brand name. Amazon founder Jeff Bezos hammered home the message when he said, "If you make customers unhappy in the physical world, they might each tell six friends. If you make customers unhappy on the Internet, they can each tell six thousand friends."[4]

It's really smart to put *at least as much* energy into satisfying your current customers as you do to win new ones. Customers are generally expensive to acquire. Do you know how much your customers cost you to acquire? If you want to increase your customer base profitably, you'll need to understand your customer acquisition cost (CAC): the total sales and marketing cost required to earn a new customer over a specific time period. And when CAC is compared against LTV (lifetime value), you'll have an even better sense of how profitable you'll be in the future after the customers have been around for a longer period of time.

My daughter Meghan works in user acquisition for a mobile gaming business. She invests her company's marketing spend on platforms like TikTok to promote the game that she is responsible for. On a basic level, she is ensuring that the CAC remains below the LTV of a user. Marketing spend is powerful, but she and her colleagues know that if the game isn't satisfying to the player, their relationship with it will be brief. There is little point in investing heavily in customer acquisition if you don't take care to value and retain those customers.

The young woman who cuts my hair has set up her own salon. Phoebe uses Instagram to show people what she can do (before and after shots) and offers new customers an incentive to come and have a first experience. It's free, and it works. The key thing is that when they come, the experience is so good they want to come back, and they refer her to others as well. Use social media, but always get the fundamentals of delivering for customers right.

My direct experience of leading a highly bespoke, client-focused B2B business taught me the following:

> Be really clear what makes a great customer for your business. For my business, they needed to be comfortable with being challenged, not just supported, for example. At the risk of overgeneralization, banking was not a sector where our approach was valued (too corporate, too profit-driven, too culturally different).

> Personalize the approach from the very beginning—it represents a taste of what is to come. The first dialogue must lay a trail for how the experience will develop and build both confidence and trust.

> Be generous in the early stages (with time, not money)—customers need a chance to get to know you; you're confident that when they do, they will value you. Penny-pinching is foolish. Protect your price positioning, though (see chapter 39).

> Do an exceptional job for the client. Provide the right people, the right project design, the right support team, and strong communication and collaboration with the client throughout. Deliver what you promise; nothing less will do. More than anything else, this is what creates satisfaction, continuation, and referrals.

> Stay in touch with people even when there is no ongoing work. Show that your interest extends long after the invoices are settled. Be human.

> Share experience through events, research, and writing—both to share your distinctive point of view and to develop your knowledge and connections. This kind of marketing may develop new clients, but it's mostly about brand building.

This approach is not going to create a fast-growth business, make no mistake. But for many companies out there, especially in the service sector, these fundamental principles work really well.

For every venture, whatever the sector, whatever stage in the business journey you're at, your customers represent your purpose in action. As leaders, we need to create an organizational culture and system that drives excellence in serving those customers.

Reflections on Managing Customers

1. Are you clear about who your customers are and what they need from you? How well designed is your product service experience for those customers?

2. Do you understand the economics of customer acquisition and retention in your business?

3. Does your company culture respect and value customers? Is everyone united in seeking to deliver an exceptional experience for them and consistently working to improve it?

4. As a leader, do you demonstrate on a daily basis your personal commitment to delivering for customers—in ways that are visible to both your team and your customers?

CHAPTER 42

Managing Partners

Co-founders will endure so much together that their relationship is often compared to a marriage.

—Jessica Livingston, a founding partner of the seed stage venture firm Y Combinator

B ack in chapter 2, I made the case for not being alone on this journey. The right partner (or partners) will add pace and energy to what you are doing. They will bring different strengths and create resilience in your organization.

Despite the benefits that come with co-founders, on the flip side, 65 percent of startups fail *because* of co-founder conflict, according to Noam Wasserman, author of *The Founder's Dilemmas*.[1] The business growth journey puts a lot of stress on co-founder relationships. Common disagreements include issues with roles and responsibilities, vision and strategic alignment, and equity and compensation. These topics of disagreement often conceal underlying relationship difficulties. Addressing a disagreement over, say, strategy may do little to change the long-term trajectory of the relationship. The conflict's roots need to be surfaced and worked through for that to happen.

In that sense, co-founder relationships are very much like marriages—I don't say this lightly, given that my wife of thirty years and I co-founded our consultancy business twenty-five years ago. Multiple relationships like this exist when you are both co-founders *and* something else; perhaps you are friends, married, or family. These types of partnerships are more complicated to navigate than pure business partnerships because if the business fails, your relationship may suffer, and if your relationship suffers, the business may fail.

When you live and breathe your business, it can leak into every conversation. My wife, Jane, and I learned from experience to separate work and home life and give each the care it deserves. It wasn't always plain sailing. At a certain point, one of those roots of conflict that I referred to needed attention. Jane ran the practice but had limited involvement in delivering client work, despite having relevant education and experience. In the early stages, she didn't feel that her contributions were seen and valued by me or the other partners. If a role is considered more or less valuable, quantifiable, or externally visible, it can lead to recurring disagreements. Jane was and is instrumental in any success that Value Partnership achieves—she deserves full recognition. She brings a strong execution energy that complements my strategic approach, as well as a lot of personal warmth and passion. It hasn't always been easy, but we are proud of how together we have navigated our family and business lives. It's chiefly because our relationship is strong, and if either of us needs to be heard, we are.

In chapter 2, I introduced Bas and Ross, the tech-savvy co-founders of Limbic AI. They mutually agreed that their respective CEO and CTO roles would have no impact on their partnership relationship, despite the apparent change in the power dynamic. They share values, trust each other, and, although highly collaborative, don't feel the need to talk about some issues now. They do connect almost daily, though. Spending informal time together regularly allows you to build and maintain your relationship. It helps to build trust and mutual understanding. You then can support each other's decisions and handle conflict more easily.

Being clear about roles is another important way to avoid unnecessary conflict or confusion, especially for colleagues. Clarify one another's roles and decision rights, not just your job titles. Each of you has an important leadership job to do. And if you use your founder card to trump decisions made by other leaders in your organization, expect there to be consequences. In one organization I worked with, two of the founders stayed in leadership roles beneath the externally hired CEO. They did not always agree with the strategy of the CEO and expressed those views openly. It meant that there was confusion about where power and authority lay— until we established some clear governance. In terms of executive authority, that must lie with the CEO. In the boardroom, the CEO is accountable to the founders/owners.

The truth is, sometimes relationships break down. Just as in a marriage when divorce is sometimes best for all parties, so it is in business. More than once, I have had to mediate a separation that enables the business, and the people involved, to move on. In one case, two co-founders had grown apart over five years. They became co-founders on the back of a strong friendship. One of the partners, who we will call Stefano, for years viewed his friend as "somewhat lazy." His partner, Lorenzo, was content for Stefano to drive things. Stefano's frustration led to him offering Lorenzo the chance to buy him out for one euro at one stage. Lorenzo refused, saying, "You're my brother." When COVID-19 struck, an energized team pivoted the business with limited contribution from Lorenzo. A key investor effectively became Stefano's partner, and they saved the business from bankruptcy with no help from Lorenzo. By this point, Stefano's frustration had mushroomed.

The catalyst for breakdown came when the team decided to invest in a new market. Lorenzo, who spoke the language, agreed to manage this "on the ground." There was no visibility of what was happening; Stefano admits he left this alone and had no intention of "rescuing" Lorenzo again. The finance manager became concerned and wanted to understand what was going on. There was no business plan, no processes, no cash forecast, no contract in place for the local manager. Lorenzo was largely absent. At this point, the relationship was broken on both a professional and a personal level.

By then, Stefano's views about Lorenzo had hardened. He wanted him out of the day-to-day business completely. While Lorenzo tried to restore his personal relationship with Stefano, Stefano was focused on untangling his business relationship with him. In collaboration with the investors, I was asked to mediate. Mediation requires a number of conditions to be in place:

> Objective feedback on the situation (interview all the "actors")

> Trust in the impartiality of the process and person

> Ground rules (e.g., honesty without careless judgment)

> A calm, safe, step-by-step process

> Regular clarifying, testing, summarizing

> Closure and actionable next steps

The result was a sale of Lorenzo's stake to Stefano at a valuation carried out by third parties and the immediate cessation of Lorenzo's involvement in the business. The personal relationship is broken, sadly.

This process was painful and time-consuming for everyone involved. Try to avoid ever getting to this point. The truth is both parties were ignoring the problems that had been building for five years. Yes, five years. They failed to talk about them until they had become deep and intractable—and the trust became broken. John D. Rockefeller, American business magnate, put it well when he said, "A friendship founded on business is better than a business founded on friendship."

Reflections on Managing Partners

1. Where is your level of trust with your co-founder(s)? Are you spending enough unstructured, informal time together?

2. Are you and others across your business clear about the roles and contributions expected of you as the founders? Are you giving the people you hire the space they need to do their jobs?

3. Is there a clear distinction between ownership and leadership in your governance arrangements?

4. If things are not going as well as you had hoped, are you sharing that, discussing it, and trying to solve problems before they become a threat to the business?

CHAPTER 43

Ensuring Good Governance

I tend to think the importance of good governance increases linearly with the size of the business and the number of shareholders.

—Robb McLarty, chief investment
officer at Flow Capital[1]

For startups, establishing a professional, independent board and other aspects of corporate governance tends to be down the priority list. But there are important ethical, legal, and fiduciary considerations for companies of *any* size. As a business grows, it creates obligations to investors and employees. The CEO needs to be held accountable, even if he or she is the majority owner. The CEO also benefits from a sounding board to hear different perspectives and have conversations about strategy and deliverables. But good governance is not just about the board—the role of management in providing good governance on a day-to-day basis is arguably just as important.

The majority of early-stage companies are led by people who haven't yet had the opportunity to learn about governance. And, let's be honest, if you're a first-time entrepreneur and business leader setting out to conquer the world, it's way more interesting to be talking about your product or how to win customers than about corporate governance. But ignore it at your peril.

In the previous chapter, I described how two co-founders—who started out as great friends—fell out, nearly bringing the business down with them. If a board had been in place, a chairperson would have been there to detect or deal with the problem before it perpetuated a crisis. Remember, the problem had been brewing for five years.

In another organization, I described how two of the four founders stayed on in operational management roles after the appointment of an external CEO. In the absence of an effective governance framework, there were multiple decision and communication channels between the board and managers in the company (partly as a consequence of the operational involvement of certain board members). Some board members viewed the executive team (ET) as insufficiently skilled in certain key areas or insufficiently focused on the performance of the core business. Employees often viewed shareholders as the "real" decision makers (not the ET). There was no clear, consistently applied CEO mandate (e.g., budget), resulting in micromanagement by some board members and detailed supervision of the CEO through frequent and long board meetings. This supervision shifted as the performance of the business or confidence in the management changed, leading to periods of truce and periods of conflict.

What were the consequences of all this? For the CEO, it was like driving with the brakes on:

> Decision-making was slowed down, convoluted, and pushed upward.

> Management accountability was ambiguous.

> Mixed messages about priorities were communicated.

> Management credibility and morale were damaged.

> Talent was lost.

To resolve the situation, shareholders accepted the need to implement a robust governance framework; their commitment is always essential to make governance work. Hand in hand with it, the executive team needed to be strengthened in key positions to increase shareholder confidence that they could delegate powers with minimal risk.

Corporate governance is not an end in itself, but rather a means of adding value and providing continuity. Governance principles should always be applied in a pragmatic and flexible manner, with regard to the individual circumstances of a company. The handover of executive responsibilities to hired managers, as in the case described, is a classic "trigger," creating a requirement for strengthening governance.

In the early days of Value Partnership, we established a board with a nonexecutive chairperson who was accountable for governance and the performance/behavior of the board. When you establish a board, it's important to reach a shared agreement about how you will work together as a board—to develop some principles such as these:

> Vision and strategy are decided as a whole board at formal board meetings.

> When a decision is made, we all uphold it 100 percent afterward.

> The CEO and leadership team are responsible for execution—the board should avoid micromanaging.

> The CEO must keep the board informed on critical developments.

> Any board director can bring evidence that a decision needs to be rethought—but only after an agreed period of supportive execution, and only in a scheduled board meeting.

> At agreed intervals, the board and leadership team meet as one group.

These principles worked for our board. I recommend that you develop your own with your own board.

Having the wrong governance structure in place is almost as bad as having no governance. One of my clients is currently struggling with a board made up of investors focused on their own needs who are not adding value to the substance of his business. The board feels like a drag rather than an enabler of business growth. He is now seeking a change of chairman and new types of contribution that would really add value, such as the experience of growing a professional service business in the United States and how to evolve the science behind their product. Make sure your board really serves your business.

Beyond the board, every business needs good management governance. That means considering what forums are required for operational and strategic management. So, for example, you might decide on weekly performance reviews, monthly strategy reviews, and quarterly team reviews. Each forum should have a clear purpose, time commitment, agenda scope, chair, and attendance. The cadence of accountability should be designed to suit your business and industry.

An effective governance framework establishes stable and accepted relationships between shareholders, the board, management, and other stakeholders. It defines an agreed distribution of power between the main players involved with the firm. Try not to see it as an unnecessary bureaucratic burden. Instead, make it work for you.

Reflections on Ensuring Good Governance

1. To what extent do you have an effective governance framework in place for your business? Is that governance framework proportionate, given the size and challenges facing your business?

2. Do you have a board, and if you do, is it adding value to the business? If not, what are you going to do about that?

3. Have you established a clear system for management accountability? What are your decision-making forums, how effective are they, and what needs to improve?

CHAPTER 44

Building a System

You do not rise to the level of your goals. You fall to the level of your systems.

—James Clear, *Atomic Habits*

"I'm going to run a marathon," I said. "That's my goal." At the time, I could run five miles, not 26.2 miles. If I was going to complete a marathon, I needed a training system. The answer was simple: Create a plan with the progress mapped out—a little more each week (10 percent is the guide)—and stick it on the side of the cupboard in the kitchen that confronts me every morning. Add a red pen, ready to check off each activity. There was no way I was going to cheat and no way I was going to miss a check mark, so I did the work. It was mainly to avoid the ignominy of failure, but also because I started to (surprisingly) enjoy it. My system worked—it was what made the goal achievable.

Businesses are like this, too. Through systems, we stack the odds in our favor. We need to *design* our businesses to deliver, not simply have a winning idea. As Will Shu, founder of Deliveroo, put it, "I am not obsessed with the idea of building a business, I am obsessed with the business I am building."[1] It is no good building a strong, emotional connection with customers if we cannot reliably deliver for them. Every idea needs a system to ensure that it works consistently well.

The truth is that winners and losers often share the same goals. I was working with one of the mobile network operators in the UK during the early 2000s and noticed that all the network operators had more or less the same vision and strategy. They were uncannily alike. Winning was going to be about who executed best, so that's what we focused our energy on. Building the best customer experience required systems designed to do that consistently and reliably. Systems help you to win, not just to deliver on your goals.

British Cycling is a perfect example of a system designed for building winners. Between 1908 and 2003, British riders had won just a single gold medal at the Olympic Games. What happened in 2003? David Brailsford was appointed performance director of British Cycling. Brailsford brought a new and relentless commitment to a strategy he referred to as "the aggregation of marginal gains," which was the philosophy of searching for a tiny margin of improvement in everything you do. As hundreds of small improvements accumulated, from the design of the bikes to the pillows the riders slept on, the results came faster than anyone could have imagined. The British cycling team won 60 percent of the gold medals available in road and track cycling at the 2008 Beijing Olympics. Four years later, in London, British cyclists set nine Olympic records and seven world records.[2]

So, how do you know what you need to systematize? Big companies tend to systematize everything, to their cost. A major Japanese-owned corporation started buying growing companies around the world to add innovative, consumer-friendly applications to their technology. But they demanded that these growing companies use the same HR, finance, and

IT systems as the parent company. You can imagine what happens when a mature company's systems are applied to a previously entrepreneurial company. It ends up strangling the golden goose while it tries to lay eggs.

Systems should be built to achieve your goals. To protect your margins, ensure good customer service, or maximize the likelihood that your marketing spend generates returns. When you think about this, consider where you need to operate more systematically. Look at your business model and ask yourself, "What needs to be efficient and consistent—and why?"

A high-end travel agency I worked with was building highly bespoke trips for their clients and struggling to ensure their margins were protected. Time-consuming research, client dialogue, and costing requests to multiple providers created huge amounts of work and complexity. They charged a "trip design fee" based on the number of travelers and the length of the trip. These factors did not reflect the work involved in designing and executing the trips. We changed their pricing model so the price was always 25 percent over the full cost of a trip. A simpler business model and a new CRM system greatly reduced the administrative burden. This system stopped squeezing the earnings of the two founders.

Here is another example, this time from the hotel industry. Dynamic pricing in hotels is a system used to improve revenue and ensure maximum occupancy for the hotel, based on supply and demand. This is also known as "time-based pricing" due to the fact that these prices are manipulated in real time based on algorithms. Such a system takes into account factors that affect market demand, such as seasonality, competitor pricing, current occupancy, consumer demands, and other external factors. The goal is to minimize the chance that a room goes unsold and to maximize the price being paid for that particular room. By using machine-learning, hoteliers can adjust their prices to meet the demand and mirror the market trends. By offering prices that meet the market value, hotels will no longer run the risk of charging less than the perceived value of the room and more than what guests are willing to pay.

So, building a system can mean a variety of things, from a consistent policy, a checklist, a formula, or an algorithm. Whatever it is, it needs to serve your business, not put unnecessary constraints on it, and move you closer to your goals. Goals are not enough; you must have the means in place to achieve them. Systems allow you to build an engine for consistent performance so you can focus on what *only* humans can do: provide creativity, inspiration, and engagement.

Reflections on Building a System

1. To what extent do you have an effective system in place to ensure the success of your business model? What does your business deliver consistently well, and what does it not?

2. How clear are you about what you now need to systematize to underpin profitable growth and the delivery of your business purpose?

3. What are the next steps that you need to take to act on your response to question 2? Who is best placed to lead this work?

CHAPTER 45

Failing Is Learning

I've missed more than nine thousand shots in my career. I've lost almost three hundred games. Twenty-six times, I've been trusted to take the game-winning shot and missed. I've failed over and over and over again in my life. And that is why I succeed.

—Michael Jordan

R ay Dalio, in his book *Principles*, says, "Over the course of our lives, we make millions and millions of decisions that are essentially bets, some large and some small. It pays to think about how we make them because they are what ultimately determines the quality of our lives."[1] You are sure to get *many* of those decisions wrong, so you had better get used to it. The key thing, then, is to be ready to try, fail, and learn. As Ray put it, "I feared boredom and mediocrity much more than I feared failure."[2]

Ray may not fear failure, but many of us do. For some, it can be crippling, and that makes trying, failing, and learning hard. This is often a learned behavior—you may have grown up in an environment where people taught you that failure was unacceptable, or that anything less than perfect was failure. Yet we know that failing is something we all have to come to terms with—and maybe even celebrate. Ideally we learn this when we are young, because it prepares us for navigating a turbulent world where uncertainty is a given and resilience is a must.

How does a fear of failure show up? Perhaps you are anxious about being judged by others or unwilling to accept constructive criticism or help. Maybe you are prone to procrastination if a task or activity seems challenging. If you don't try, you can't fail, right? This is not a behavior that sits well with the demands of being a founder. Despite this, many leaders still struggle with failure, *especially* those with highly successful education and career track records. Getting straight As in college examinations, where there is a right answer, does not prepare you for life when even the questions are undefined.

Also, sometimes failure isn't failure; it's a feeling. A leader made redundant because of a major organizational realignment couldn't shake the perception that he himself had somehow failed, even though there was nothing he could have logically done to change this outcome.

How can we let go of this stigma and anxiety about failure? One way is to define success better—or more realistically. Setting an unattainable goal, not qualified by your actual experience, is a surefire way of coming up short when, in fact, you've probably outperformed. A four-hour marathon runner setting a three-hour goal but finishing in three hours and thirty minutes is only a "failure" by their own definition.

Another way is to set what are sometimes called *approach* goals rather than *avoidance* goals. With avoidance goals, we aim to avoid failure—for example, to stop procrastinating. Approach goals aim to achieve positive outcomes such as strengthening our leadership capability. Research suggests that our "well-being" is enhanced by pursuing approach goals rather than avoidance goals.[3]

When coaching clients are uncertain, I sometimes ask them to make three lists: (1) the worst-case scenario, (2) things that could prevent the failure, and (3) in the event of failure, what could be done. Next, I ask them to write down the benefits of the attempted effort and the cost of inaction. This exercise often helps people to crystalize the cost of *not* acting—and makes the risks seem more worthwhile. (Refer back to chapter 29 on making decisions.)

There is little doubt that failure comes with collateral damage. We don't fear it irrationally. When failure happens, it can make us fearful and fill us with doubt, sadness, even despair. Fortunately, these feelings are usually transient. What matters is how we respond to failure and what we learn. In my work as a coach, I find myself helping leaders to confront situations like this honestly—I become an accountability partner and help them to learn. Failure teaches us resilience. In a way, failure is the very essence of entrepreneurship.

A good example of this is the process of customer development in startups. The aim is to put a minimum viable product in the hands of customers. You want to understand how they will interact with it. Some founders struggle to issue such a product because they worry that it isn't ready. But the more tough feedback you get, the better. Ask the questions that might kill the product. Fear nothing. Failure generates insights. You want a bad idea to fail as fast as possible. The last thing you want is false praise and a product that won't survive in the real marketplace. Failure saves wasted effort and underpins a successful outcome from customer development. Instagram is a case in point. It launched in 2010 as a location-sharing application. Today it is a social media platform with over two billion monthly active users. In other words, over time its unique value proposition has been transformed.[4]

The lean startup movement has made invalidating, updating, and upgrading your "hunch" *the* way to build a technology business.[5] "Pivoting" is no longer seen as a failure—it has become a founder's badge of honor. Every leader needs to consider the value of this way of thinking, acting, and learning. It requires perseverance to identify a great idea, coupled with a strong belief in what you are trying to do.

Traditional businesses that have been around a long time often get cluttered up with systems and processes that no longer add value. Peter Drucker, in his book *Management Challenges for the 21st Century*, wrote about what he called *organized abandonment*, meaning we should put everything on trial for its life on a regular basis. The question to be asked is this: "If we did not do this already, would we, knowing what we now know, go into it?" If the answer is "no," the next question must be "What do we do now?"[6] Sometimes, in order to make progress, we need to stop things, not just start doing new things.

Finally, if we want to destigmatize failure and create an environment in which failure is recognized for what it is—the evidence of risk taking and learning—we need to value it rather than punish it. Every failure is a valuable lesson, so focus on the lesson. It's a sign that you've stepped far enough out of your comfort zone to try something different. Ultimately, that will help you to rise and thrive.

Reflections on Failing Is Learning

1. Do you have a fear of failure? If so, why do you think that's the case? How does that impact you?

2. What would help you to step outside your comfort zone and take more risks? What is success—have you clearly defined it? What risks are you taking by trying to avoid failure?

3. What can you learn from the lean startup movement mantra "fail fast"? How could that mindset help you to move forward with greater conviction?

4. What are you doing to create a working environment in which members of your team can take risks and innovate without fear? And where learning from failure is celebrated?

CHAPTER 46

Keeping Things Simple

Simplicity and sincerity generally go hand in hand, as both proceed from a love of truth.

—Mary Wollstonecraft, author

I was asked to help a company work on their strategy and was looking through various internal documents as I considered how best to help. I came across their key performance indicators (KPIs). It was two pages long with 110 indicators. I nearly fell off my chair. When I asked about this, the response was, "That's why we have a list of *key* KPIs." Even that list had more than twenty indicators on it. I was momentarily speechless. Human nature is such that we seem to complicate things. Perhaps we think it shows off our abilities, sophistication, and intelligence. One thing it does not do is add value.

According to a 2017 study by the University of Lausanne, published in the *Journal of Applied Psychology*, high intelligence can make you a better leader, but only up to a point—the brightest among us are, in fact, less-good leaders. Reinforcing the findings of previous studies, the researchers found a positive correlation between intelligence and leadership abilities, but only up to an IQ of about 120, from which point the correlation started reversing. The researchers couldn't be sure of exactly why the brightest people were worse leaders than their less intelligent counterparts, but they suggested that it could be because they are more likely to use complex language, are less skilled at simplifying tasks, and struggle to see what others find difficult or challenging.[1]

My experience suggests that the researchers are right. Very bright people frequently overcomplicate things because they see and may very well understand the complexity. But the perfect answer may not be the best one and it may take too long to reach that conclusion. The 80:20 rule teaches us that.

Great leaders have an uncanny knack of cutting through complexity rather than creating it. A famous example of this is the way Steve Jobs simplified the Apple product lineup on his return to the company in 1997. At that time, Apple had many different products designed for multiple segments. In his biography, author Walter Isaacson describes the moment when, after weeks of meetings, Jobs drew a simple grid on the whiteboard. A desktop and portable computer for the consumer and professional segments—just four products.[2]

But Jobs didn't stop there. Richard Rumelt describes Apple's turnaround in his book *Good Strategy/Bad Strategy*: "Within a year, things changed radically at Apple. Although many observers had expected Jobs to rev up the development of advanced products, or engineer a deal with Sun, he did neither. What he did was both obvious and, at the same time, unexpected. He shrunk Apple to a scale and scope suitable to the reality of its being a niche producer in the highly competitive personal computer business. He cut Apple back to a core that could survive."[3]

The value of focus has been long known and frequently forgotten. William of Occam, an English Franciscan friar who lived from 1287 to

1347, made a famous contribution to philosophy that has become known as Occam's razor. The razor metaphor is a problem-solving principle that "entities are not to be multiplied without necessity."[4] In other words, the simplest solution to a problem is usually the best one.

Cleverness is not the only barrier to simplicity. Excessive inclusion creates problems, too. A client shared their strategy with me. All of the execution is under eight pillars, each of which has a high-level purpose, goals, and action log. The five-year goals are not really goals; there is no clear or measurable destination. There are many abstractions and principles rather than tangible commitments. It is long and wordy. Digging deeper, I realized that the strategy represents an unresolved set of strategic questions about what the vision for the company really is. It does not inspire, clarify, or create urgency. It complicates and slows the business down. Metaphorically speaking, it's like artery-clogging excess cholesterol in the bloodstream. The only reason the business is getting away with this is the long-term value of its core brand and the loyalty of its customers.

The Hedgehog and the Fox is a famous essay published as a book in 1953 by philosopher Isaiah Berlin. In it, Berlin divided thinkers into two categories: hedgehogs and foxes. This classification is a reference to a saying of the ancient Greek poet Archilochus: "The fox knows many things, but the hedgehog knows one big thing." Hedgehogs have a single grand idea that they apply to everything, while foxes come up with a new idea for every situation. Jim Collins, in a 2001 *Fast Company* article, said, "All good-to-great leaders, it turns out, are hedgehogs. They know how to simplify a complex world into a single, organizing idea—the kind of basic principle that unifies, organizes, and guides all decisions."[5]

Compound interest is a powerful principle—a small amount of money can grow into large amounts over time if left alone. The story goes that Albert Einstein called compound interest the most powerful force in the world. Focus compounds even faster than money. Not enough focus leads to diminishing returns. Therefore, set no more than three goals. Champion no more than three values. Recognize two basic types of decisions. One minimum viable product. Simplify what you offer customers. Make pricing easy to do and understand. The lesson of simplicity is peppered throughout this book.

Consulting companies sometimes organize around both client partners and operating partners. The former secures and manages the relationship; the latter ensures successful delivery of the project(s). What happens when you remove the distinction and they work together as one team? A client did just that and gave each partner a client relationship to focus on. The partners are collaborating better (none of the old handoffs are necessary), they feel that they can do better work being much more focused, clients are happier, and sales are improving sharply.

Simplicity, success, and a great customer experience go together; when you keep things simple, they tend to be robust—less goes wrong, and there is less to maintain and less to break down. Simplicity leads to accuracy, reliability, and lots of "up time."

Reflections on Keeping Things Simple

1. What is your capability to keep things simple? If you struggle in this area, are you surrounding yourself with people who are talented at this?

2. When you think about your business, how clear and focused is it? Is it more like a hedgehog or a fox?

3. If you wanted to simplify your business and organization, what would make the biggest difference and why? Fewer strategic priorities? A simpler organization design? A more straightforward customer offer? Or . . . ?

CHAPTER 47

Staying Flexible

Stay committed to your decisions, but stay flexible in your approach.

—Tony Robbins, from a LinkedIn post

When Queen Elizabeth II visited the London School of Economics during the global financial crisis of 2008, she reportedly asked, "Why did no one see it coming?" Good question. The vast majority of people involved in the financial industry refused to believe that anything could go wrong. House prices would continue to rise no matter what . . . until they didn't.

As an outsider, I have seen many leadership teams become so locked into their view of the world that they cannot process suggestions that they might be wrong. This is sometimes called *confirmation bias*—we look for evidence that supports our view and discard anything that doesn't. In a team setting, we call it *groupthink*.

A good example is Swissair, once renowned for its financial stability. Due to high levels of liquidity, it was once known as the "flying bank." During the 1990s, overconfidence and hubris led to a series of bad decisions, which eventually caused the airline to collapse. Foremost of these bad decisions was the ill-advised "hunter strategy" in which the airline attempted to expand by buying up smaller airlines. It bought stakes in numerous loss-making airlines, including Belgium's Sabena and Poland's Lot, in an attempt to form its own airline alliance and give themselves easier access to the European market. The airline found itself overwhelmed by debt and quickly became insolvent.

Flexibility is the willingness to change or compromise. But before we find ourselves in a crisis, it makes a lot of sense to bake in flexibility, both in our minds and our organizations. For that, we need to be prepared to see things we may prefer not to see, unlike the leadership of Swissair.

My own business has operated on a virtual basis since it was founded in 1998. We've never felt the need for a status office, particularly given that the bulk of our work time was spent in client offices around the world. We were already set up for working from home. It didn't matter where our team lived, and our cost base was low and carefully controlled. When the pandemic struck, we only had to learn how to consult using online technology. Flexibility was already largely baked in.

In her book *The Scout Mindset*, Julia Galef explores two very different mindsets: that of the soldier and that of the scout.[1] Most of us have a soldier mindset—we cling to our beliefs and often ignore evidence that might prove us wrong. But, she argues, we can all learn to be scouts, seeking out truth and improving our "map" of the world. One of the reasons we are so reluctant to diverge from the views of the group is that we fear being ostracized. Dissenters are often viewed as difficult people. Scouts believe that the best way of getting to the truth is to be prepared to be wrong. It's a bit like testing out a minimum viable product to find out what isn't right about it.

Being an "outsider" gives me permission to dissent on significant issues to a degree that insiders rarely feel. I can ask questions about or highlight things I see going on in the business that appear to make no sense. Often, they appear to make no sense because they make no sense. I can often tell that insiders agree and have been waiting for the opportunity to speak up. We need to create a culture in which it isn't necessary to have an outsider around for this to happen.

Leaders need to go out of their way to foster dissenting views, to encourage others to name risks that are being missed. To make it comfortable to disagree, not just in strategy workshops but in everyday dialogue as well. It can be useful to systematize such dissention and make it a part of the culture.

I did some consulting work with parts of Serco back in their heyday in the 2000s. I found they had a rigorous internal process whereby all new bids and proposals had to be "black-hatted" in conferences, during which hardened public service managers were invited to challenge the optimistic bidding assumptions made by the financial teams at headquarters. This referred to Edward de Bono's thinking caps idea, where the black hat is the hat of logic and critical judgment. Black-hat thinking encourages a group to consider any weak points in an idea or solution and figure out how to avoid or counter them.

However, a subtle but noticeable shift in the company's priorities began in the mid-2000s. Under CEO Chris Hyman, Serco steadily became obsessed by its own financial performance. He set the company an internal goal of joining the FTSE 100 list of the UK's largest companies, which it achieved in December 2008. During the depths of the global economic downturn, in 2010 the company then set a new goal— to become "the world's greatest service company"—and issued ambitious forecasts for revenue growth and profits by 2012. Chasing these targets in the face of austerity in the UK and the federal shutdown in the United States meant expanding into new areas, such as clinical healthcare and large-scale private outsourcing, which Serco had avoided in the past. The risks increased sharply. And one of the principal defenses against poor decision-making—the black-hat conferences—either did not take place, or became formalities, dominated by bid teams. Serco survived, just—but their story serves as a reminder of the damage that an unbridled profit motive can do to the culture of a business.

A business needs to be ready for changes in the environment—to embrace rather than resist them. If we are purpose-led, we will pivot to pursue that purpose whenever necessary. We will not be held back by a short-term hit to the bottom line. We will do strategically what we need to do to win. Given the huge range of uncertainties in the global economy, flexibility is at a premium. The pandemic dealt a blow to inflexible businesses. Others have pivoted and thrive still.

That level of flexibility starts with you, the leader. It starts with a scout mindset, a readiness to consider risks, be less attached to the status quo, and less attached to your own habits. It means building flexibility into your organization, including flexible people, flexible working, flexible processes, and a flexible structure. If you find yourself surrounded by people who all agree on the important issues, ask yourself if that feels right. The people you surround yourself with shape your identity. As Julia Galef says, "In the medium-to-long term, one of the biggest things you can do to change your thinking is to change the people you surround yourself with."[2]

Reflections on Staying Flexible

1. What is your mindset? Are you a soldier or a scout?

2. When you think about your team, how ready are you to explore risks and consider radical alternatives? Do team members feel able to speak up about the need to change course?

3. To what extent have you baked flexibility into your organization, strategy, and culture?

CHAPTER 48

Telling Stories

You can have the best technology, you can have the best business model, but if the storytelling isn't amazing, it won't matter. Nobody will watch.

—Jeff Bezos[1]

Stories change how we see the world. They carry in them our cultural identity. It's said that Alexander the Great learned to read and write by studying Homer's *Iliad* as a young man, guided by the philosopher Aristotle. When he embarked on his conquests, Homer's story of an earlier Greek expedition to Asia Minor served as a blueprint, and he stopped at Troy, even though the city had no military significance, to reenact scenes from the *Iliad*. For the entire duration of his conquest, he slept alongside his copy. And of course, he wrote his own story into history.

Storytelling is the art of using fact and narrative to imbue understanding. Michael Harris, writing in the *Harvard Business Review* in 2015, says, "If you want to influence how a customer feels about your product, provide an experience that creates the desired emotion. One of the best ways for a customer to experience your complex product is by sharing a vivid customer story."[2] Research has shown that stories can activate the region of the brain that processes sights, sounds, tastes, and movement.[3]

"Organizational psychologist Peg Neuhauser found that learning which stems from a well-told story is remembered more accurately, and for far longer, than learning derived from facts and figures. Similarly, psychologist Jerome Bruner's research suggests that facts are twenty times more likely to be remembered if they're part of a story."[4]

The evidence is clear: Stories evoke emotions. They bring theories and information to life. They are memorable in a way that facts and figures are not. Contrast a presentation of the last period's financial results with hearing the CEO tell the story of that period—the big wins, the challenges, the people who made it happen. Which would you rather listen to? Good stories often contain multiple meanings so they're surprisingly economical in conveying complex ideas in ways that are easy to grasp. A dry recitation of data points simply fails to communicate.

Storytelling is everywhere in business—the best leaders know how to tell stories. Watch Steve Jobs tell the story of the first iPhone at its launch back in 2007. It is a masterpiece in storytelling, and his audience is captivated. A pitch is the story you tell investors. A brand is the story you tell customers. Your story is why someone may choose to be led by you.

You might think that investors are deeply rational and data driven. But the truth is they are as influenced by their emotions as anyone else. Their herd mentality, their fear of missing out, and their intuition may override their cold calculations, so we should act with that understanding in mind. Your ability to describe how your modest company will become a giant should have all the ingredients of a brilliant story.

What is the best way to tell a story? One very helpful model to consider is Think, Feel, Do. The following is based on the writing of Emily Taylor Gregory:[5]

> *Think:* What do you want your audience to think about your proposition?

> *Feel:* What emotional response do you expect from your audience and how do you want them to feel about your proposition?

> *Do:* What action do you want your audience to take?

Using this approach will make your story more powerful and ensure that it addresses not just the logical but also the emotional and behavioral responses you would like to see.

In his 2011 book *Thinking, Fast and Slow*, psychologist Daniel Kahneman challenges the view that people make decisions based on the logical processing of critical information. Kahneman argues that there are two different processes or modes of thought at work: "System 1" is fast, instinctive, and emotional; "System 2" is slower, more deliberative, and more logical. System 2, in Kahneman's scheme, is our consciously effortful mode of reasoning about the world. System 1, by contrast, is our largely unconscious mode. It is System 1 that detects impatience in a voice and effortlessly interprets familiar patterns. It is System 2 that swings into action when we have to fill out a form or park a car in a tight space.[6]

Kahneman's theory helps us to understand the Think and Feel components of the Think, Feel, Do model. However, capturing your audience's attention with a powerful headline and holding their interest with insightful content is all very well, but if you don't make the next step clear to them, the Do, how will you influence their behavior?

One of my clients, Roger, storyboards everything he does. He applies the Think, Feel, Do model to all his stakeholder relationships. Not surprisingly, he has a fantastic track record selling B2B services to C-level clients. I have also observed him sitting around a campfire telling his founding story to his team. He needed no slides and only one prop: the 1997 McKinsey book *The War for Talent*. It so infuriated him at the time that he set up his business Chemistry as the antidote to that way of thinking about talent. Roger's story is great because it has purpose and passion behind it and because we all love an underdog, a hero to root for. Now he is equipping the partners in his firm to be the best storytellers they can be to replicate his success and contribute further to the growth of Chemistry.

Which brings me to Pixar. Pixar is arguably one of the greatest storytellers of our generation. Over the years, they've won countless Academy Awards, Golden Globes, and Grammys. Here are some of their twenty-two rules for storytelling:

> Great stories are universal (part of the human condition).

> Great stories have a clear structure and purpose: Once upon a time, there was [blank]. Every day, [blank]. One day, [blank]. Because of that, [blank]. Until finally [blank].

> Great stories have a character to root for (an underdog).

> Great stories appeal to our deepest emotions.

> Great stories are surprising and unexpected.

> Great stories are simple and focused.[7]

Try applying these rules the next time you have a significant presentation to make. Effective storytelling involves a deep understanding of human emotions, motivations, and psychology in order to truly move an audience.

Leadership storytelling is not just useful for raising finances or selling to clients. It also helps you lead your organization authentically. Sharing your personal story helps your team to understand who you are as a leader. If your team understands you better, it leads to greater trust. Storytelling is a flexible tool that allows you to convey lessons, instill your organization's values, and acknowledge your team's contributions.

Reflections on Telling Stories

1. What is your approach to communication? Are you a storyteller or do you simply share information?

2. When you think about your approach to communicating, how much energy do you typically invest in each element of Think, Feel, and Do? What could you learn from Pixar's rules?

3. Considering your different stakeholders (investors, customers, team), where do you need to work harder and do better in how you tell your story?

CHAPTER 49

Saying Goodbye

What do you plan to do after Entelo?

—an interview question asked by
John Bishke, founder and ex-CEO of Entelo

Y ou may find John Bishke's question odd. Before an employee has even joined, he's already asking about what's next on their growth path. But Culture Amp® research consistently shows that one of the strongest drivers of engagement is when people feel they have the opportunity to gain experience and develop. Having the conversation to understand where somebody wants to go and showing them how you can help makes them feel valued. Let's face it, we are well past the days when employees joined a company and intended to stay until retirement. Counterintuitively, doing everything you can to help them get to where they want to go can actually mean they stick around longer.

Didier Elzinga, founder and CEO of Culture Amp®, puts it this way: "My job as a leader is not to keep people forever; it's to keep them for as long as they are in the best place for both them and for Culture Amp. By actively engaging in that conversation, I find I can stretch that period of time because I'm more actively involved in their development."[1]

People will leave—either because they want to, or because you want them to, or because, reluctantly, you have to let them go. Either way, the most important thing is, if at all possible, to say goodbye well. We are going to explore each of these situations and why that matters.

People tell you that they are leaving. If you are unlucky, it's just at the moment you're counting on them to deliver something business-critical. This is often hard for founders because they cannot imagine giving up on their purpose and vision. But for others, their business may be a stepping stone. The best people perform well and are consequently desirable to others. When they leave, it's easy to feel betrayed or let down. I felt this when a key member of our team left, largely because of circumstances. But you have to be accepting and move on, fast. You want them to talk well about you as a leader and an employer, wherever they go. There's nothing to gain from forcing them to serve every last drop of their notice, for example. Explore what you honestly can learn from their exit. Don't avoid difficult messages because they are hard to hear or because you are disappointed in them. If I am honest, though, I have always struggled with this.

Then there are those employees with whom you decide you have reached the end of the line, perhaps because they are not performing or are having a corrosive impact on the culture of your firm. These situations should be managed according to the law, of course, and in line with your company's HR policies and values. Any failure to do these three things will hurt you. Managing such employee exits well can have significant benefits, including reducing the costs associated with employee turnover, protecting your reputation so you can still attract talent, avoiding legal disputes, and protecting morale. I'm not going to explore how to handle firing an employee here; there are countless resources available elsewhere on this management skill. But I do want to highlight two things.

First, too many leaders wait far too long before acting on difficult people decisions, hoping that things can be turned around. Sometimes they can, and we should try to achieve that outcome. But we also should be really clear on what good performance is, really straight with our feedback on actual performance, really supportive on improvement efforts—and we should put a time limit on the decision period. That forces us to both ramp up our commitment to solving the problem and avoid prevarication. Why? Because very often that person's poor performance has a serious effect on their team and peers. For example, let's say a newly appointed senior leader is not transitioning well into management. They still behave like an individual contributor, micromanage team members, and don't recognize the need to show empathy or support to their team. Morale slumps, people feel mistrusted, and eventually team members start leaving. Inaction in this situation can become very costly indeed.

Second, beware of the hidden costs of downsizing. Even though productivity rises in the short term as fewer workers cover the same volume of work, the impact on the "survivors" carries demonstrable costs. As well as declines in job satisfaction and engagement, survivors show a 20 percent drop in job performance. Charlie Trevor of the University of Wisconsin–Madison and Anthony Nyberg of the University of South Carolina found that downsizing a workforce by 1 percent leads to a 31 percent increase in voluntary turnover the next year.[2] Recent data by Culture Amp highlights the detrimental impact of layoffs on the employee experience.[3] When layoffs happen, remaining employees don't feel "lucky" to still have a job. Rather, they lose motivation, pride, commitment, and faith in the company and its leadership. Not to mention, one-third of those left willingly walk out the front door, taking with them knowledge, expertise, culture, and continuity. Organizations will not fully recover until around twelve to eighteen months post-layoffs. That's a long time to endure declining levels of engagement and the adverse effect they have on people and profit.

So, before laying off even small numbers of employees for what seems like sensible cost reasons, consider *all* the costs and look for creative alternatives. The wrong reason for layoffs is to achieve short-term cost cuts. The right reason might be long-term strategic change or an existential threat to the firm. Regardless, leaders should remember that layoffs will have grave consequences.

With that existential threat in mind, some situations leave us with nothing left to do but to lay off substantial numbers of people. Perhaps the business is simply running out of cash or is otherwise unsustainable. We have to face this sometimes as leaders; it is our responsibility. Pete Harold, a good friend of mine, faced this situation in 2016 and 2017. His story is instructive, if tough.

Within days of 9/11, Panoramic Resources was floated to raise funds for a processing plant and open-pit nickel mine at Savannah, in the Kimberley region of Western Australia. Pete was the first managing director and a shareholder. He wanted to build a great long-term business that took care of its people. Mining began in late 2004. In 2005 Panoramic purchased and restarted the Lanfranchi Nickel Project, an underground mine near Kambalda, a seven-hour drive from Perth. By 2008, the business employed 450 people and had a peak market capitalization of $1.2 billion Australian dollars with significant cash in the bank. In April 2007, the price of nickel peaked. It never reached those heights again. It bounced back in 2010 and 2011, only to fall steadily until 2016. The historically low USD nickel price forced the board to make an extremely tough decision. The Lanfranchi and Savannah Projects were placed on "care and maintenance" in November 2015 and May 2016 respectively. Each site shutdown cost two hundred jobs, with more lost at the headquarters in Perth.

The board and executive team felt that mining and selling nickel from the asset at low prices was unsustainable and against the interests of shareholders. Pete faced up to the unenviable task of talking to groups of thirty to forty workers at a time. At one point, in his car on the way to one of the sites, he pulled over, having second thoughts. He spoke to his CFO, and they agreed it was the right thing to do. Pete looked his workers in the eye and told them the truth about the situation. He promised to honor their settlement terms. He helped people find new positions where he could. The fact that the company had been well managed, had a strong culture, and had trust between management and the workforce made this process easier than it would otherwise have been. As I said, the most important thing is, if at all possible, to say goodbye well.

Pete knows that leadership brings with it unenviable responsibility. The decision to place the mine on care and maintenance was one he presented to the board, and they supported it. But the decision, and the consequences of it, are still with him today, seven years later. It impacted his sleep for years, replaying over and over in his mind. He often second-guesses his decision. The nickel price started climbing within a year, thanks to the diesel emissions crisis and the growth in electric vehicle demand. Very recently, he bumped into one of his old team. She told him that Panoramic was the best place she had ever worked because of the culture Pete was instrumental in creating. It also helps him to know that most of his old team are in good jobs and doing just fine these days.

All we can do as leaders is our best. Even when it comes to saying goodbye.

Reflections on Saying Goodbye

1. How do you handle people who choose to leave the company? Are you ready to let them go and can you move on quickly?

2. When you think about your approach to managing poor performance, do you deal with it with professionalism? Are you protecting your company values and making decisions that reinforce them?

3. When faced with significant economic headwinds, have you done everything creatively possible to avoid layoffs? And if layoffs are genuinely unavoidable, how can you do it with as much integrity, empathy, and generosity as possible?

CHAPTER 50

Enjoying the Journey

Treating different things the same can generate as much inequality as treating the same things differently.

—**Kimberlé Crenshaw,** civil rights advocate and author

In my thirties, I received a job offer from a top US investment bank. They offered to pay me more money than I had ever imagined earning at the cost of working very long hours and traveling constantly. However, the true cost would have been missing the early years of my daughter's life, her first steps, her first day at nursery school, her first everything. I said no and founded my own company instead. I wanted purpose, values, family, and independence more than I wanted money. Your work is one of the pillars that defines your life. Choose to do something that feels worthwhile to you and do it in a way that is aligned with your values. Make time for loved ones. Take care of your physical and mental health. Wealth will never compensate for an absence of those things, in my experience.

So much for my choices. What are yours? You are unique, a complete one-off. Which brings us right back to the early chapters of this book, especially chapter 3 (managing your energy) and chapter 5 (identifying your default patterns). Know yourself well enough to make good decisions for you. As serial entrepreneur and author Richie Norton puts it, "Forget work-life balance. . . . Do the thing you want and create systems to support that. Perfectly imbalanced in the direction you want to go is perfectly acceptable."[1] Your priorities change throughout your life, so what looks like a good balance will change, too. There is no perfect balance—only the right choices for you at this point in your life.

Founders create the vast majority of new jobs, pull economies out of recessions, introduce useful products and services, and create prosperity. That's a lot of "heavy lifting." A recent study from the University of San Francisco found that founders are more likely to experience mental health problems than people who don't own their own businesses. In fact, 72 percent of entrepreneurs participating in the study reported mental health problems—particularly anxiety and depression.[2]

Pete Harold's story in the last chapter reminds us that leadership is hard—sometimes very hard. In a notoriously cyclical industry, 450 hard-won jobs came and went. But Pete is resilient. He's back in the hot seat of another resourcing company, looking to restart an old nickel mine to create wealth and jobs again and providing the raw materials for the growth in electric vehicle demand. Panoramic is back mining nickel, too.

As author Marcus Buckingham points out in his book *Love and Work*, you need to love what you do because "loveless work" leaves you psychologically damaged eventually.[3] And loveless daily work can't compensate for having a strong purpose. Marcus reckons we need to enjoy *at least* 20 percent of the time we spend working—moments when we feel "in flow." For me, that's working with a leader or a team on something that really matters to them, helping them generate new insights and conviction about what they need to do next. That's a low-altitude thing, whereas purpose is a high-altitude thing.

You don't need to create a unicorn to consider yourself a success. And the speed, risk, and energy required to achieve that level of success is extremely demanding of the founder. In terms of capital raising, we are no longer in a growth-at-all-costs environment in which sales growth is rewarded above all else. Profitability is back in fashion. Very few venture capital–backed businesses that have gone public in the last fifteen years are profitable. My consulting company, while not scalable, still grew and has always been profitable. Some have called it a *lifestyle business*—a term I've always bridled at. Whatever you call it, my family and others have prospered and enjoyed our work (well, most of the time!). In my experience, having worked with many founders, it is important not to take on a level of risk that sits uneasily with who you are. If you have family depending on you, the stakes are high. You are taking that risk on their behalf. What's your level of risk aversion?

Founders are, almost by definition, very driven people. In their book *The Molecule of More*, Daniel Z. Lieberman and Michael E. Long explore how the brain chemical dopamine kindles our desires and fuels our creativity.[4] Scientists think that our brain divides the world into two separate regions: near and far. Everything that's close to us—the things we can touch, see, and feel at any given moment—falls into the "near" category. Anything that's out of our immediate reach—figuratively or literally—falls into the "far" category. Dopamine gets you excited about the things that fall into the "far" category and motivates you to pursue them. It encourages a hunter to track that elusive animal, or an entrepreneur to launch that new venture.

Unfortunately, dopamine can never be satisfied, no matter how well things are going for us in any given moment. Fortunately, our brain isn't *only* governed by dopamine. It is also governed by other chemicals: serotonin, oxytocin, endorphins, and endocannabinoids. These chemicals allow us to derive pleasure from the present moment. A "dopaminergic" person may tend to avoid the present and become consumed by all the possibilities the future holds. They become so immersed in the world of their imagination that they forget to savor the present. And that is to their loss.

So, as you go on this journey, try not to be so obsessed with the destination that you fail to appreciate the moments. A big new client win. A great team performing at their best. Seeing people growing around you. And appreciate the tough moments, too. Sprinting through London, late for a meeting. Breaking down at a team Christmas dinner. Stuck in the snow at Dulles Airport. Finding a way through COVID-19. All these moments are the snapshots of your life; they are where you learn and grow.

As a leader, you can't always be the good guy; sometimes you have to confront and share bad news. Invest in the relationships around you—your team, your clients, your investors—and you will build a well of goodwill. You'll need to call on this at times. If you can be yourself, be honest with those around you, and be true to your purpose, you'll be just fine.

Success—what is it, really? Being married and still in love with my wife after thirty years. Having a daughter I could not be prouder of who is on her own journey now. And though I have passed my sixtieth birthday, I am still young at heart, with a voracious appetite for learning. I still have work to do in the world, unfinished business.

Reflections on Enjoying the Journey

1. Do you have a chance to play to your strengths every day?

2. Are you taking care of yourself and your family?

3. Can you enjoy the journey, not just focus on the endgame?

Jan Bolz, Simon Court, and Rob Small in 2016.

Acknowledgments

could not have written this book without my amazing wife and business partner, Jane. This is also her story.

My Value Partnership colleagues and friends contributed a great deal to the learning captured in this book, especially Geoff Rogers, who helped me to build the practice; Bruce Slatton, who continues our work; friend and advisor David Shaw; and my ever-present support Karen Lewis.

The Greenleaf team believed in my book from the first moment. First Justin Branch, then Brian Welch and editor Tess Newton guided it through the publishing process with great expertise and good grace. And special thanks to Emma Price and Kirsten Levermore for helping to get the book in good shape when I first started writing.

My clients and partners gave me the opportunity to fulfill my purpose in life and taught me much. They are too numerous to mention by name, but they all shaped this book in a sense. I do want to call out and thank those who contributed to the book directly: Rob and Jan, the unicorn builders; Roger Philby; Pete Harold; Eli Bressert; Bas De Vries; Gary Macbeth; Didier Elzinga; and the team at The GC Index®.

A special mention for Rachel Page who bet a month's salary on me, a brave woman!

Finally, as a coach I have been blessed with my own mentors for much of my working life. Nickie Fonda, Don Young, and Charlotte Chambers all taught me so much about leadership, why it matters, and how to practice it with integrity.

Notes

INTRODUCTION

1. Arthur C. Brooks, *From Strength to Strength: Finding Success, Happiness, and Deep Purpose in the Second Half of Life* (Middlesex, UK: Portfolio, a division of Penguin Random House, 2022).

2. Ray Dalio, *Principles: Life and Work* (New York: Simon & Schuster, 2017).

3. Carol Dweck, *Mindset: The New Psychology of Success* (New York: Random House, 2007).

4. Matthew Syed, *Bounce: The Myth of Talent and the Power of Practice* (London: 4th Estate, 2011).

5. Marie Forleo, *Everything Is Figureoutable* (New York: Penguin, 2019), 120-122.

6. Paul Polman and Andrew Winston, *Net Positive: How Courageous Companies Thrive by Giving More Than They Take* (Boston: Harvard Business School Publishing, 2021).

7. Polman and Winston, *Net Positive*.

CHAPTER 2

1. Quoted in Alice Bentinck and Matt Clifford, *How to Be a Founder: How Entrepreneurs Can Identify, Fund, and Launch Their Best Ideas* (London: Bloomsbury Business, 2022), 99.

2. Elon Musk, "Elon Musk: On Team Building, Warren Buffet and Mars (Transcript)," Fresh Dialogues, interview with Alison van Diggelen, February 9, 2023, https://www.freshdialogues.com/2013/02/09/transcript-of-elon-musk-interview-with-alison-van-diggelen-on-team-building-warren-buffett-and-mars/.

3. Elon Musk, "50 Innovation and Success Quotes from SpaceX Founder Elon Musk," written by Larry Kim, *Inc.*, March 8, 2016, https://www.inc.com/larry-kim/50-innovation-amp;-success-quotes-from-spacex-founder-elon-musk.html.

4. Caleb Naysmith, "Bill Gates Reveals Warren Buffett's Life-Changing Advice to 'Hang Out with People Better Than You,'" Yahoo! Finance, June 5, 2023, https://finance.yahoo.com/news/bill-gates-reveals-warren-buffetts-174800717.html.

5. Jason Greenberg and Ethan R. Mollick, "Sole Survivors: Solo Ventures Versus Founding Teams," *SSRN*, January 2018, http://dx.doi.org/10.2139/ssrn.3107898.

6. Travis Howell, Christopher Bingham, and Bradley Hendricks, "Don't Buy the Myth that Every Startup Needs a Co-Founder," *Harvard Business Review*, April 2022, https://hbr.org/2022/04/dont-buy-the-myth-that-every-startup-needs-a-co-founder.

CHAPTER 3

1. Peter F. Drucker, *Management: Tasks, Responsibilities, Practices* (New York: Harper Collins, 1993).

2. Tony Schwartz and Catherine McCarthy, "Manage Your Energy, Not Your Time," *Harvard Business Review*, October 2007, https://hbr.org/2007/10/manage-your-energy-not-your-time.

3. Johann Hari, *Lost Connections: Why You're Depressed and How to Find Hope* (New York: Bloomsbury, 2018).

4. Peter Senge, *The Dance of Change: The Challenges to Sustaining Momentum in Learning Organizations* (New York: Bantam Doubleday Dell, 2004), 82-87.

5. Peter Senge, *The Fifth Discipline Fieldbook: Strategies and Tools for Building a Learning Organization* (New York: Crown, 1994), 312-326.

6. Shonna Waters, PhD, "Manage Your Energy, Not Your Time: How to Work Smarter and Faster," *BetterUp* (blog), September 10, 2021, https://www.betterup.com/blog/manage-your-energy-not-your-time.

CHAPTER 4

1. Roselinde Torres, "What It Takes to Be a Great Leader," TED, October 2013, https://www.ted.com/talks/roselinde_torres_what_it_takes_to_be_a_great_leader?language=en.

2. Mark S. Granovetter, "The Strength of Weak Ties," *American Journal of Sociology* 78, no. 6 (1973): 1360–80, http://www.jstor.org/stable/2776392.

3. Ian Leslie, "Why Your 'Weak-Tie' Friendships May Mean More Than You Think," *The Life Project* (blog), BBC, July 2, 2020, https://www.bbc.com/worklife/article/20200701-why-your-weak-tie-friendships-may-mean-more-than-you-think.

CHAPTER 5

1. Daniel Goleman, *Emotional Intelligence: Why It Can Matter More Than IQ* (New York: Random House, 2005).

2. David Zes and Dana Landis, "A Better Return on Self-Awareness," The Korn/Ferry Institute, August 2013, https://www.kornferry.com/content/dam/kornferry/docs/article-migration/KFI-SelfAwareness-ProofPoint-6.pdf.

3. The GC Index®, https://www.thegcindex.com.

CHAPTER 6

1. Angela Duckworth, *Grit: The Power of Passion and Perseverance* (New York: Scribner, 2018).

2. Randy Cohen, Chirag Bavishi, and Alan Rozanski, "Purpose in Life and Its Relationship to All-Cause Mortality and Cardiovascular Events: A Meta-Analysis," *Psychosomatic Medicine* 78, no. 2 (February–March 2016), doi: 10.1097/PSY.0000000000000274, 122–33.

3. See Celeste Leigh Pearce, PhD, MPH, quoted in "Association Between Life Purpose and Mortality Among US Adults Older Than 50 Years," JAMA Network, May 24, 2019, https://jamanetwork.com/journals/jamanetworkopen/fullarticle/2734064?utm_source=For_The_Media&utm_medium=referral&utm_campaign=ftm_links&utm_term=052419.

4. Mihaly Csikszentmihalyi, *Flow: The Psychology of Optimal Experience* (New York: Harper Perennial Modern Classics, 2008).

CHAPTER 7

1. Brené Brown, *Dare to Lead: Brave Work. Tough Conversations. Whole Hearts.* (New York: Random House, 2018).

2. Elon Musk, "Elon Musk's Full Speech at the 2017 International Astronautical Congress," Go To Space, September 29, 2017, YouTube video, 44:07, https://www.youtube.com/watch?v=cj3OgrvvBpE.

3. A DuPont leader shared this during a presentation and subsequent discussion I attended.

CHAPTER 8

1. Jim Collins, *Good to Great: Why Some Companies Make the Leap . . . and Others Don't* (New York: HarperBusiness, 2001).

2. Amy Y. Ou et al., "Humble Chief Executive Officers' Connections to Top Management Team Integration and Middle Managers' Responses," *Administrative Science Quarterly* 59, no. 1 (January 2014), https://doi.org/10.1177/0001839213520131.

3. Amy Y. Ou et al., "Do Humble CEOs Matter? An Examination of CEO Humility and Firm Outcomes," *Journal of Management* 44, no. 3 (September 21, 2015), https://doi.org/10.1177/0149206315604187, 1147–73.

4. Edgar H. Schein, *The Power of Relationships, Openness, and Trust* (Oakland, CA: Berrett-Koehler Publishers, 2018).

5. Amy C. Edmondson, "How to Turn a Group of Strangers into a Team," TED Talk, June 14, 2018, YouTube video, 13:07, https://www.youtube.com/watch?v=3boKz0Exros.

6. Rodger Dean Duncan, "Ken Blanchard: Why Servant Leadership Requires Humility," *Forbes*, May 8, 2019, https://www.forbes.com/sites/rodgerdeanduncan/2019/05/08/ken-blanchard-why-servant-leadership-requires-humility/?sh=46d25eac25f2.

7. Rick Warren, *The Purpose Driven Life: What on Earth Are We Here For?* (Grand Rapids, MI: Zondervan, 2012).

8. Adam Grant, *Think Again: The Power of Knowing What You Don't Know* (New York: Viking, 2021), 48.

9. Tomas Chamorro-Premuzic, "Why Humble Leaders Are Rare," *Forbes*, June 29, 2020, https://www.forbes.com/sites/tomaspremuzic/2020/06/29/why-humble-leaders-are-rare/?sh=4179ca7f649b.

CHAPTER 9

1. Charlotte Alter, "How Whitney Wolfe Herd Turned a Vision of a Better Internet into a Billion-Dollar Brand," March 19, 2021, *Time*, https://time.com/5947727/whitney-wolfe-herd-bumble/.

2. Alter, "How Whitney Wolfe Herd Turned a Vision."

3. *Nelson Mandela: Prisoner to President* directed by Peter Davis (Villon Films, January 1, 1994).

CHAPTER 10

1. Dr. Julie Smith, *Why Has Nobody Told Me This Before?* (New York: HarperOne, 2022).

2. Dr. Lynda Folan, "Defining Resilience and How It's Key to Changing Your Business for the Better," *People Management*, September 2022, https://www.peoplemanagement.co.uk/article/1797728/defining-resilience-its-key-changing-business-better.

3. Roselinde Torres, "What It Takes to Be a Great Leader," TED, October 2013, https://www.ted.com/talks/roselinde_torres_what_it_takes_to_be_a_great_leader?language=en.

CHAPTER 11

1. Chris Zook and James Allan, *The Founder's Mentality: How to Overcome the Predictable Crises of Growth* (Boston: Harvard Business Review Press, 2016).

2. Dr. Ichak Adizes, *Managing Corporate Lifecycles* (Santa Barbara County, CA: Adizes Institute, 2004).

3. Andrew Hill, "The Torment of Founders Who Cannot Let Go of Their Babies," *Financial Times*, https://www.ft.com/content/e8a7454e-5172-11e9-9c76-bf4a0ce37d49.

4. Noam Wasserman, "Rich Versus King: The Entrepreneur's Dilemma," *Academy of Management Proceedings* 2006, no. 1 (August 2006), https://doi.org/10.5465/ambpp.2006.22896807.

5. Wasserman, *"Rich Versus King."*

6. Original tweet/memo from Jack Dorsey that he sent to his employees on Twitter, November 29, 2021, https://twitter.com/jack/status/1465347002426867720.

7.   Reid Hoffman, "If, Why, and How Founders Should Hire a 'Professional,'" LinkedIn, January 23, 2013, https://www.linkedin.com/pulse/20130123161202-1213-if-why-and-how-founders-should-hire-a-professional-ceo/.

CHAPTER 12

1.   Warren Buffett, "Berkshire Hathaway Inc.: 2014 Annual Report," Berkshire Hathaway Inc., 2015, https://www.berkshirehathaway.com/2014ar/2014ar.pdf.

2.   Lex Donaldson and James H. Davis, "Stewardship Theory or Agency Theory: CEO Governance and Shareholder Returns," *Australian Journal of Management* 16, no. 1 (June 1991), https://doi.org/10.1177/031289629101600103.

3.   Patagonia, "Patagonia's Next Chapter: Earth Is Now Our Only Shareholder," Patagonia, September 14, 2022, https://www.patagoniaworks.com/press/2022/9/14/patagonias-next-chapter-earth-is-now-our-only-shareholder.

4.   Companies Act, 2006, c. 2, sec. 172 (Eng.), https://www.legislation.gov.uk/ukpga/2006/46/contents.

CHAPTER 13

1.   Boonsri Dickinson, "Ben Horowitz: Founders Should Learn How to Be CEO," *Insider*, March 21, 2012, https://www.businessinsider.com/ben-horowitz-2012-3.

CHAPTER 14

1.   Pearl Zhu, "Five Strengths of Innovation Leaders," October 1, 2019, Innovation Management, https://innovationmanagement.se/2019/10/01/five-strengths-of-innovation-leaders/.

CHAPTER 15

1.   Whitney Wolfe Herd quoted in Elle Morris, "Uncovering White-Space Opportunities for Your Brand," *Forbes*, December 11, 2019, https://www.forbes.com/sites/forbesagencycouncil/2019/12/11/uncovering-white-space-opportunities-for-your-brand/?sh=60998e077b60.

2. Ben Horowitz, *The Hard Thing About Hard Things: Building a Business When There Are No Easy Answers* (New York: Harper Business, 2014).

CHAPTER 16

1. Roselinde Torres, "What It Takes to Be a Great Leader," TED, October 2013, https://www.ted.com/talks/roselinde_torres_what_it_takes_to_be_a_great_leader?language=en.

2. Chris Moran, "EA Makes Worst Company in America History, Wins Title for Second Year in a Row!" Consumerist, April 9, 2013, https://consumerist.com/2013/04/09/ea-makes-worst-company-in-america-history-wins-title-for-second-year-in-a-row/.

3. Ian Scherr, "How Electronic Arts Stopped Being the Worst Company in America," CNET, June 2, 2015, https://www.cnet.com/tech/gaming/how-electronic-arts-stopped-being-the-worst-company-in-america/.

CHAPTER 17

1. Jeroen De Flander, *The Art of Performance: The Surprising Science Behind Greatness* (Netherlands: The Performance Factory, 2019).

2. "2020 Zeno Strength of Purpose Study," Zeno Group, June 17, 2020, https://www.zenogroup.com/insights/2020-zeno-strength-purpose.

3. Leigh Buchanan, "What's Next for Toms, the $400 Million For-Profit Built on Karmic Capital," *Inc.*, accessed September 17, 2023, https://www.inc.com/magazine/201605/leigh-buchanan/toms-founder-blake-mycoskie-social-entrepreneurship.html.

4. Greg Roumeliotis, "Exclusive: TOMS Shoes Creditors to Take Over the Company," Reuters, December 27, 2019, https://www.reuters.com/article/us-tomsshoes-m-a-creditors-exclusive-idUSKBN1YV1PT.

5. Nicole Motter, "A Look Inside the 6 Types of Social Enterprises," SOCAP Digital, August 29, 2017, https://bthechange.com/a-look-inside-the-6-types-of-social-enterprises-fd51331d47de.

CHAPTER 18

1. Richard Branson, "Do well by doing good," Twitter, May 24, 2017, https://twitter.com/richardbranson/status/867338186237898756.

2. Francesca Gino, "To Motivate Employees, Show Them How They're Helping Customers," *Harvard Business Review*, March 6, 2017, https://hbr.org/2017/03/to-motivate-employees-show-them-how-theyre-helping-customers.

3. Irena C. Grugulis and Adrian Wilkinson, "Managing Culture at British Airways: Hype, Hope, and Reality," *Long Range Planning* 35, no. 2 (2002): 179–94, http://dx.doi.org/10.1016/S0024-6301(02)00036-5.

4. Dan Cable, "Helping Your Team Feel the Purpose in Their Work," *Harvard Business Review*, October 22, 2019, https://hbr.org/2019/10/helping-your-team-feel-the-purpose-in-their-work.

CHAPTER 19

1. James Heskett, *The Culture Cycle: How to Shape the Unseen Force that Transforms Performance* (Upper Saddle River, NJ: FT Press, 2012).

2. Patrick Lencioni, *The Advantage: Why Organizational Health Trumps Everything Else in Business* (San Francisco: Jossey-Bass, 2012).

3. "Join Chemistry," The Chemistry Group, accessed August 28, 2023, https://www.thechemistrygroup.com/join-chemistry.

CHAPTER 20

1. David Cummings, "The Top 3 Things Every Entrepreneur Needs to Know," David *Cummings on Startups* (blog), December 7, 2011, https://davidcummings.org/2011/12/07/the-top-3-things-every-entrepreneur-needs-to-know/.

2. Edgar H. Schein with Peter A. Schein, *Organizational Culture and Leadership* (Hoboken, NJ: John Wiley and Sons, Inc., 2016), 183.

3. Chaman Nahal, *People and Performance: The Best of Peter Drucker on Management* (Delhi: Allied Publishers, 1988), 120.

4. David Cummings, "The Hallway/Zoombomb Values Test," *David Cummings on Startups* (blog), August 15, 2020, https://davidcummings.org/category/leadership/.

5. "Netflix Culture—Seeking Excellence," Netflix, accessed September 17, 2023, https://jobs.netflix.com/culture.

CHAPTER 21

1. Richard Rumelt, *Good Strategy/Bad Strategy: The Difference and Why It Matters* (London: Profile Books, 2011).

2. John Greathouse, "5 Time-Tested Success Tips from Amazon Founder Jeff Bezos," *Forbes*, April 30, 2013, https://www.forbes.com/sites/johngreathouse/2013/04/30/5-time-tested-success-tips-from-amazon-founder-jeff-bezos/?sh=1f09eb93370c.

CHAPTER 22

1. Ram Charan, Larry Bossidy, and Charles Burck, *Execution: The Discipline of Getting Things Done* (New York: Currency, 2002).

2. Thomas Carlyle, *The Life of Friedrich Schiller: Comprehending an Examination of His Works* (New York: Charles Scribner's Sons, 1901), 45, https://www.google.com/books/edition/The_Life_of_Friedrich_Schiller/r8o0YOdWePsC?hl=en&gbpv=1.

3. Chris McChesney, Sean Covey, and Jim Huling, *The 4 Disciplines of Execution: Achieving Your Wildly Important Goals* (New York: Simon & Schuster, 2012, 2021).

CHAPTER 23

1. Colin Bryar and Bill Carr, *Working Backwards: Insights, Stories, and Secrets from Inside Amazon* (New York: St. Martin's Press, 2021).

2. Gareth Morgan, *The Art of Creative Management* (Thousand Oaks, CA: Sage Publications, 1993).

3. Jamil Qureshi, "Psychologist Reveals How to Hack Your Brain for Success," *The Diary of a CEO*, produced by Steve Bartlett, December 21, 2020, YouTube video, 1:05:25, https://www.youtube.com/watch?v=prw1xtkdfhs.

4. Henrik Kniberg, "Spotify Engineering Culture," produced by Andreas Tjernsli, February 27, 2017, YouTube video, 13:12, https://www.youtube.com/watch?v=4GK1NDTWbkY.

CHAPTER 24

1. Susan Galer, "Global Study: Barely 16% of Companies Ready for Digital Leadership," *Forbes*, September 1, 2016, https://www.forbes.com/sites/sap/2016/09/01/global-study-barely-16-of-companies-ready-for-digital-leadership/?sh=63d68051d05b.

CHAPTER 25

1. Peter Drucker, *Management Challenges for the 21st Century* (New York: Harper Business, 2001).

CHAPTER 26

1. Magnus Sverke, Johnny Hellgren, and Katharina Näswall, "No Security: A Meta-Analysis and Review of Job Insecurity and Its Consequences," *Journal of Occupational Health Psychology* 7, no. 3 (July 2002): 242–64, https://doi.org/10.1037/1076-8998.7.3.242.

CHAPTER 27

1. "The Top 12 Reasons Startups Fail," CB Insights, August 3, 2021, https://www.cbinsights.com/research/report/startup-failure-reasons-top/.

CHAPTER 28

1. Friedrich Nietzsche, *Basic Writings of Nietzsche*, trans. and ed. Walter Kaufman (New York: Modern Library, 2000), 226.

2. Rachel Makinson, "How Spanx Founder Sara Blakely Created a Billion-Dollar Brand," *CEO Today*, October 28, 2021, https://www.ceotodaymagazine.com/2021/10/how-spanx-founder-sara-blakely-created-a-billion-dollar-brand/.

3. Hannah L. Miller, "Sara Blakely: 7 Life Lessons from the founder of SPANX," Leaders, November 18, 2021, https://leaders.com/articles/women-in-business/sara-blakely-spanx/.

4. Laura Huang, *Edge: Turning Adversity into Advantage* (New York: Portfolio, an imprint of Penguin Random House, 2020).

CHAPTER 29

1. Ray Dalio, Principles: *Life and Work* (New York: Simon & Schuster, 2017), 524–29.

2. Dalio, *Principles*, 283.

3. Jeffery P. Bezos, "Exhibit 99.1," Letter to Shareholders, Amazon.com, accessed August 28, 2023, https://www.sec.gov/Archives/edgar/data/1018724/000119312516530910/d168744dex991.htm.

4. Bezos, "Exhibit 99.1."

CHAPTER 30

1. Daniel Goleman, *Emotional Intelligence: Why It Can Matter More Than IQ* (New York: Random House, 2005), xv.

2. Tara Van Bommel, "The Power of Empathy in Times of Crisis and Beyond," Catalyst, 2021, https://www.catalyst.org/reports/empathy-work-strategy-crisis/.

3. Daniel Goleman, "How Emotionally Intelligent Are You?" LinkedIn, April 21, 2015, https://www.linkedin.com/pulse/how-emotionally-intelligent-you-daniel-goleman/.

CHAPTER 31

1. Janine Kruger and Chantal Rootman, "How Do Small Business Managers Influence Employee Satisfaction and Commitment?" *Acta Commercii* 10, no. 1 (December 6, 2010), https://doi.org/10.4102/ac.v10i1.114.

2. David Wee and Handi Kurniawan, *Great Advice for Solving Everyday Challenges at Work and in Life* (Hong Kong: Hong Kong Open Page Publishing Company Limited, 2022), 156.

3. Alfie Kohn, *Punished by Rewards: The Trouble with Gold Stars, Incentive Plans, A's, Praise, and Other Bribes* (New York: Houghton Mifflin Harcourt Publishing, 1999).

4. Lindsay McGregor and Neel Doshi, *Primed to Perform: How to Build the Highest Performing Cultures Through the Science of Total Motivation* (New York: Harper Business, 2015).

CHAPTER 32

1. David H. Maister, Charles H. Green, and Robert M. Galford, *The Trusted Advisor* (New York: Free Press, 2000), 69.

2. Shoshanna Delventhal, "How Jeff Bezos Became One of the World's Richest People," Investopedia, May 24, 2023, https://www.investopedia.com/investing/how-jeff-bezos-got-be-worlds-richest-man/.

CHAPTER 33

1. Patrick Lencioni, *The Five Dysfunctions of a Team: A Leadership Fable* (San Francisco: Jossey-Bass, 2002).

2. Lawrence Serewicz, "RBS vs. Lehman Brothers Failures in Leadership, Culture, and Regulators," *Thoughts on Management* (blog), June 26, 2012, https://thoughtmanagement.org/2012/06/26/rbs-vs-lehman-brothers-failures-in-leadership-culture-and-regulators/.

3. Jim Collins, Good to Great: *Why Some Companies Make the Leap . . . and Others Don't* (New York: HarperBusiness, 2001), 74.

CHAPTER 34

1. Ram Charan, "The Secrets of Great CEO Selection," *Harvard Business Review*, December 2016, https://hbr.org/2016/12/the-secrets-of-great-ceo-selection.

2. Shannon Shaper, "How Many Interviews Does It Take to Hire a Googler?" re:Work, April 4, 2017, https://rework.withgoogle.com/blog/google-rule-of-four/.

3. "Why the Onboarding Experience Is Key for Retention," *Gallup Blog*, accessed September 17, 2023, https://www.gallup.com/workplace/235121/why-onboarding-experience-key-retention.aspx.

NOTES

CHAPTER 35

1. Colin Fisher, Teresa Amabile, and Julianna Pillemer, "How to Help (Without Micromanaging)," *Harvard Business Review*, January/February 2021, https://hbr.org/2021/01/how-to-help-without-micromanaging.

CHAPTER 36

1. Jinseok Chun, Joel Brockner, and David de Cremer, "People Don't Want to Be Compared with Others in Performance Reviews. They Want to Be Compared with Themselves," *Harvard Business Review*, March 22, 2018, https://hbr.org/2018/03/people-dont-want-to-be-compared-with-others-in-performance-reviews-they-want-to-be-compared-with-themselves.

2. Marcus Buckingham, "The Check-In Conversation," *Marcus Buckingham* (blog), February 15, 2018, https://www.marcusbuckingham.com/check-in-conversation/.

3. David Rock, Josh Davis, and Beth Jones, "Kill Your Performance Ratings," *Strategy+Business*, August 8, 2014, https://www.strategy-business.com/article/00275.

4. Gilbert Brim, *Ambition: How We Manage Success and Failure Throughout Our Lives* (Lincoln, NE: IUniverse.com, 2000).

5. Mihaly Csikszentmihalyi, *Finding Flow: The Psychology of Engagement with Everyday Life* (New York: Basic Books, 2008).

CHAPTER 37

1. Tomas Chamorro-Premuzic, "Why Do So Many Incompetent Men Become Leaders?" *Harvard Business Review*, August 22, 2013, https://hbr.org/2013/08/why-do-so-many-incompetent-men.

2. Mary Abbajay, "What to Do When You Have a Bad Boss," *Harvard Business Review*, September 7, 2018, https://hbr.org/2018/09/what-to-do-when-you-have-a-bad-boss.

3. Sara Morris, "Lack of Career Development Drives Employee Attrition," Gartner.com, September 25, 2018, https://www.gartner.com/smarterwithgartner/lack-of-career-development-drives-employee-attrition.

4. "The Grow Model," Performance Consultants, accessed September 17, 2023, https://www.performanceconsultants.com/grow-model.

5. Matthew Syed Consulting, "6 Most Frequently Asked Questions About Bounce," Matthew Syed Consulting, November 7, 2017, https://www.matthewsyed. co.uk/6-most-frequently-asked-questions-bounce-matthew-syed/.

CHAPTER 38

1. Bernard Coleman, "Six Leadership Fundamentals from Michael Jordan," *Inc.*, May 23, 2020, https://www.inc.com/bernard-coleman/six-leadership-fundamentals-from-michael-jordan.html.

2. Scott Keller and Mary Meaney, *Leading Organizations: Ten Timeless Truths* (New York: Bloomsbury, 2017).

3. Jon Katzenbach and Douglas Smith, *The Wisdom of Teams: Creating the High-Performance Organization* (Boston: Harvard Business Review Press, 2015).

4. Carolyn Dewar, Martin Hirt, and Scott Keller, "The Mindsets and Practices of Excellent CEOs," McKinsey & Company, October 25, 2019, https:// www.mckinsey.com/capabilities/strategy-and-corporate-finance/our-insights/ the-mindsets-and-practices-of-excellent-ceos.

CHAPTER 39

1. Ernest Hemingway, *The Sun Also Rises* (New York: Scribner, 2014), 109.

2. Michael Stier, "Speeding Along but Out of Gas (Cash)," Focus CFO, October 2021, https://www.focuscfo.com/blog/speeding-along-but-out-of-gas-cash.

CHAPTER 40

1. Lewis Hower, "Balancing the Art of Valuation with the Science of Dilution," *Tech Stars*, June 28, 2021, https://www.techstars.com/the-line/advice/balancing-the-art-of-startup-valuation-with-the-science-of-dilution.

2. Blake Masters and Peter Thiel, *Zero to One: Notes on Startups, or How to Build the Future* (London: Ebury Publishing, 2014), 86.

3. Tim Young, "Maintaining Control of Your Company: What All Founders Should Know," *Forbes*, June 23, 2019, https://www.forbes.com/sites/timyoung/2019/06/ 23/maintaining-control-of-your-company-what-all-founders-should-know/ ?sh=688460b957a5.

NOTES

CHAPTER 41

1. Catherine Morin, "How the Ritz-Carlton Creates a 5 Star Customer Experience," CRM.org, December 13, 2019, https://crm.org/articles/ritz-carlton-gold-standards.

2. "Experience Is Everything: Here's How to Get It Right," PwC, 2018, https://www.pwc.com/us/en/advisory-services/publications/consumer-intelligence-series/pwc-consumer-intelligence-series-customer-experience.pdf.

3. Fred Reichheld, "Prescription for Cutting Costs," Bain & Company, accessed September 17, 2023, https://media.bain.com/Images/BB_Prescription_cutting_costs.pdf.

4. Daniel Newman, "Customer Experience Is the Future of Marketing," *Forbes*, October 13, 2015, https://www.forbes.com/sites/danielnewman/2015/10/13/customer-experience-is-the-future-of-marketing/?sh=eb4ae19193d5.

CHAPTER 42

1. Noam Wasserman, *The Founder's Dilemmas: Anticipating and Avoiding the Pitfalls that Can Sink a Startup* (Princeton, NJ: Princeton University Press, 2012).

CHAPTER 43

1. Robb McLarty and Sean O'Dowd, "Even Small Businesses Need Corporate Governance," *Yale Insights*, January 7, 2020, https://insights.som.yale.edu/insights/even-small-businesses-need-corporate-governance.

CHAPTER 44

1. Will Shu, "Deliveroo Founder: From £0 to £5 Billion," July 12, 2021, in *The Diary of a CEO*, produced by Steven Bartlett, podcast, MP3 audio, 85:00, https://open.spotify.com/episode/1Jwdhpgd4PDKbUHL0kozE4.

2. James Clear, *Atomic Habits* (New York: Avery, an imprint of Penguin Random House, 2018), 13–14.

CHAPTER 45

1. Ray Dalio, *Principles: Life and Work* (New York: Simon & Schuster, 2017), 3.

2. Dalio, *Principles.*

3. Bridget Grenville-Cleave, "Goal-Setting Secrets," *Positive Psychology News,* January 31, 2012, https://positivepsychologynews.com/news/bridget-grenville-cleave/2012013120696.

4. "3 MVP App Examples that Are Now Massive Successes," Clearbridge Mobile, accessed September 17, 2023, https://clearbridgemobile.com/3-mobile-app-mvps-massive-success/.

5. See https://theleanstartup.com. See also Eric Reiss, *The Lean Startup: How Today's Entrepreneurs Use Continuous Innovation to Create Radically Successful Businesses* (New York: Crown Business, 2011).

6. Peter Drucker, *Management Challenges for the 21st Century* (New York: Harper Business, 2001).

CHAPTER 46

1. John Atonakis, Robert J. House, and Dean Keith Simonton, "Can Super Smart Leaders Suffer from Too Much of a Good Thing? The Curvilinear Effect of Intelligence on Perceived Leadership Behavior," *Journal of Applied Psychology* 102, no. 7 (2017): 1003–21, https://doi.org/10.1037/apl0000221.

2. Walter Isaacson, *Steve Jobs* (New York: Simon & Schuster, 2011).

3. Richard Rumelt, *Good Strategy/Bad Strategy: The Difference and Why It Matters* (New York: Crown Publishing Group, 2011).

4. "Occam's Razor," Britannica, updated August 15, 2023, https://www.britannica.com/topic/Occams-razor.

5. Jim Collins, "Good to Great," *Fast Company,* September 30, 2001, https://www.fastcompany.com/43811/good-great.

CHAPTER 47

1. Julia Galef, *The Scout Mindset: Why Some People See Things Clearly and Others Don't* (New York: Portfolio/Penguin, 2021).

2. Galef, *The Scout Mindset.*

CHAPTER 48

1. Natalie Jarvey, "Amazon's Hollywood Shopping Cart Secrets," *The Hollywood Reporter*, July 15, 2015, https://www.hollywoodreporter.com/tv/tv-features/amazon-prime-day-hollywood-shopping-808533/.

2. Michael D. Harris, "When to Sell with Facts and Figures, and When to Appeal to Emotions," *Harvard Business Review*, January 26, 2015, https://hbr.org/2015/01/when-to-sell-with-facts-and-figures-and-when-to-appeal-to-emotions.

3. Gerry Everding, "Readers Build Vivid Mental Simulations of Narrative Situations, Brain Scans Suggest," Medical Xpress, January 26, 2009, https://medicalxpress.com/news/2009-01-readers-vivid-mental-simulations-narrative.html.

4. Vanessa Boris, "What Makes Storytelling So Effective for Learning?" *Leading the Way* (blog), Harvard Business Publishing, December 20, 2017, https://www.harvardbusiness.org/what-makes-storytelling-so-effective-for-learning/.

5. Emily Taylor Gregory, "Think, Feel, Do: How to Use Rational and Emotional Content to Get an Audience Response," *Thought Leadership Blog*, FT Longitude, accessed September 17, 2023, https://longitude.ft.com/think-feel-do-how-to-use-rational-and-emotional-content-to-get-an-audience-response/.

6. Daniel Kahneman, *Thinking, Fast and Slow* (New York: Farrar, Straus, and Giroux, 2011).

7. 42courses, "PIXAR's 22 Rules of Storytelling," Medium, July 2, 2018, https://42courses.medium.com/pixars-22-rules-of-storytelling-dc24162fe8ce.

CHAPTER 49

1. Didier Elzinga, "From Our CEO: Helping Our Best Employees Grow and Go," *Culture Amp* (blog), accessed September 17, 2023, https://www.cultureamp.com/blog/helping-employees-grow.

2. Charlie O. Trevor and Anthony J. Nyberg, "Keeping Your Headcount When All About You Are Losing Theirs: Downsizing, Voluntary Turnover Rates, and the Moderating Role of HR Practices," *The Academy of Management Journal* 51, no. 2 (April 2008): 259–76, http://www.jstor.org/stable/20159508.

3. Kelly Luc and Fresia Jackson, "Employee Engagement: What to Expect After Layoffs," *Culture Amp* (blog), accessed September 17, 2023, https://www.cultureamp.com/blog/employee-engagement-after-layoffs.

CHAPTER 50

1. Richie Norton, *Anti-Time Management: Reclaim Your Time and Revolutionize Your Results with the Power of Time Tipping* (New York: Hachette Books, 2022).

2. Michael A. Freedman, MD, et al., "Are Entrepreneurs 'Touched with Fire'?" Michael Freeman, updated April 17, 2015, https://www.michaelafreemanmd.com/Research_files/Are%20Entrepreneurs%20Touched%20with%20Fire%20(pre-pub%20n)%204-17-15.pdf.

3. Marcus Buckingham, *Love and Work: How to Find What You Love, Love What You Do, and Do It for the Rest of Your Life* (Boston: Harvard Business Review Press, 2022).

4. Daniel Z. Lieberman and Michael E. Long, *The Molecule of More: How a Single Chemical in Your Brain Drives Love, Sex, and Creativity—and Will Determine the Fate of the Human Race* (Dallas, TX: BenBella Books, 2018).

Index

About the Author

Author photograph by
Mateo Villanueva Brandt

SIMON COURT has worked as a leadership coach and guide to business founders, leaders, and leadership teams for more than twenty-five years. He has a huge breadth and depth of experience across sectors, cultures, and businesses at different stages of maturity, from startup to reinvention. The sectors include entertainment, gaming, biotechnology, technology, travel, insurance, and venture capital. The cultures span the globe. The businesses are private, backed by venture capital or private equity, or are publicly owned.

He supports CEOs and their teams—first to understand their challenges, then to help the team to address them effectively. Through coaching, Simon has helped numerous leaders to grow, find their conviction, and strengthen their leadership practice. His work as a guide includes building leadership teams, developing new growth strategies, and creating organizations that can deliver with pace and agility.

While much of Simon's work is done behind closed doors, his clients will vouch for his influence and impact. He is a two-time unicorn builder.

He helped transform Miniclip into a spectacular success story over the last ten years. He also contributed to creating one of Germany's first tech unicorns, Tipico.

Simon founded the Value Partnership business with his wife, Jane. That experience as a founder informs this book and makes his empathy for founders and leaders genuine.

His qualifications include an MBA from Warwick Business School and an MSc from Imperial College. Simon is a husband, father, runner, and skier.

simon.court@value-partnership.com

www.value-partnership.com

www.linkedin.com/in/simoncourt/

Printed in Great Britain
by Amazon

39608870R00182